God Wants You Happy

FROM SELF-HELP
TO GOD'S HELP

Father Jonathan Morris, 1972-

HarperOne
An Imprint of HarperCollinsPublishers

HarperOne

The names and identifying characteristics of individuals discussed in this book have been changed to protect their privacy.

All quotations by Mahatma Gandhi have been taken from www.mkgandhi.org.

HarperCollins books may be purchased for educational, business, or sales promotional use. For information please write: Special Markets Department, HarperCollins Publishers, 10 East 53rd Street, New York, NY 10022.

HarperCollins website: http://www.harpercollins.com

HarperCollins®, 📖®, and HarperOne™ are
trademarks of HarperCollins Publishers

FIRST EDITION

Library of Congress Cataloging-in-Publication Data
Morris, Jonathan.
God wants you happy : from self-help to God's help / Jonathan Morris. — 1st ed.
p. cm.
ISBN 978-0-06-191356-3
1. Spirituality. 2. Christianity and other religions—New Age movement.
3. Happiness--Religious aspects—Christianity. I. Title.
BV4501.3.M6737   2011
248—dc22   2010053602

11 12 13 14 15   RRD(H)   10 9 8 7 6 5 4 3 2 1

I would have dedicated this book to my mom and dad—
Bob and Sharon Morris—who still teach me daily by their lives
what genuine happiness is, in the easy times and in the hard times,
but I know that they would prefer I dedicate it to you, the reader,
with a prayer that you too might become the happy, healthy,
and holy people God so wants you to be.

CONTENTS

INTRODUCTION

Spirit-Filled Living

My new butcher friend, Moe, looked at me, first with surprise, then with a broad smile. "Don't I wish!" he said, raising his thinning gray eyebrows while shuffling backward and successfully catching my freshly ground beef from his 1950s-style meat grinder without ever taking his eyes off me. The tone and mannerisms of this streetwise octogenarian from Brooklyn couldn't have expressed more skepticism over my suggestion, made to him just seconds before, that he might be on the road to becoming a saint, not altogether unlike the Italian namesake of whom he was so proud.

My sense was that this gentleman *was* on such a path; his smile was pure and real. He was spirit-filled.

Living saints were on my mind that Saturday morning as I did my neighborhood errands, because they were the topic of the scripture readings for the next day's services. During my own prayer time that morning, I had been just as surprised as Moe by the idea—so clearly expressed in the Bible—that we are *all* called to be saints and that being saints has less to do with halos and folded hands and more to do with living life to the full—becoming everything God created us to be. The message of the various readings was summed up for me in Jesus's words in the Gospel of John: "I have come that they may have life, and have it to the full" (John 10:10, NIV).

In an epiphany explicable only by divine intervention, on that day, when I had first meditated on scripture and then encountered Moe, this very familiar passage—one I had read or heard hundreds of times before—jolted me to the core. *God wants me and everyone around me to be profoundly happy!* Becoming holy and becoming happy are interconnected, I realized. And God must have a plan—and a few backup plans too, for when we mess up—outlining how we are to get there!

The moment was more than an intellectual realization. In an immeasurably short flash of reason and spiritual emotion, I knew experientially what before I had known mostly in the head: God is on my side, and his invitations, his commands, and even the bumps and bruises he permits along the way must be signposts pointing toward personal fulfillment—*life to the full*—waiting to be claimed by me and every one of God's children.

This discovery (something so obvious and simple it can hardly be called a discovery outside my own subjective experience) most likely made such a deep impression on me on that day because it contrasted so starkly with what I had been experiencing the previous week. I had been through some particularly rough days. I was dealing with my own issues of adjusting to living in New York City and serving in a Manhattan parish after many years in the more subdued and controlled environment of a seminary in Rome, Italy. My impression was that everyone around me also seemed to be going through tough times, and they weren't making much sense of their struggles. I was hurting a bit, yes, but these people were miserable. I recall the young, fearful, and inconsolable mother in the hospital with late-stage ovarian cancer; another dear friend of mine at her wits' end, frustrated and angry that she was reaching forty and still hadn't found a decent guy; an usher in my church laid off from his job one week before his wedding; a Protestant pastor and friend whose wife was leaving him for her wealthy boss; a father of three young children, suffering from debilitating and humiliating depression; and finally, the ninety-eight-year-old man at whose funeral service I presided that was attended by *nobody*—not a single person!

Over the years of my pastoral ministry I've unconsciously formed an ultrathin but steely guard that allows me to be interested in, and even immersed in, others' problems without being overwhelmed emotionally. That week, however, just beneath my serene exterior floated major doubts about God's questionable strategy of care for some of his children: "Are there real, true, positive solutions for *their* predicaments, for *every* predicament?" I wondered.

The very simple, unexceptional flash of spiritual enlightenment I experienced on that Saturday morning immediately put these concerns—summarized in my question to God about real solutions for everyone—back into life's big picture. It is a context where spiritual realities (including heaven, grace, and redemption) are taken into account. True, the previous week I had encountered a group of people who were in agony, tragically stuck in their misery, but here, through Moe's indomitable joy (even as his local butcher shop was teetering on extinction on account of new, corporate giants in the neighborhood) and through scripture, I was being reminded by grace of God's promise to us: he will bring out of every bad situation, out of every single instance of pain and suffering in our lives, a greater good—yes, an even greater good than the goodness we are missing now—if we let him! This promise covers every stripe and strand of our seemingly limitless human capacity for physical, emotional, and spiritual agony. Yes, there are real, true, positive solutions for you and for me, right now, no matter what's going on. These solutions feel like joy, peace, and profound meaning when we find them, based on hope in a God who knows us, loves us, and has great things in store for us and for the ones we love.

I've seen this promise fulfilled in the most unlikely of cases. I've witnessed people with every reason to give up, with no solution (imagined or real) in sight, reject the lie that sometimes hope is stupid and irrational, and jump up instead and move on to wonderful new chapters in their lives. I've witnessed people stuck in bad relationships and weighed down by self-destructive habits decide that today they have the grace to overcome what has beaten them for many years. In fact, whenever I am paying attention, I see myriads of everyday saints—spirit-filled people—claiming this happiness at every perilous and thorny twist and turn. The difference between these people with the ultimate success stories (overcoming difficulty and achieving happy, holy lives) and the ones who plod on in self-absorbed misery is miniscule. The divine promise of goodness is within our reach, today.

So how do we grasp it? How do we recover or acquire for the first time a heart that wakes up peacefully and goes to bed smiling?

Surely happy people can teach us something. Why is Moe still smiling, inside and out, while his little butcher shop is hanging on for dear life? Why isn't he bitter that Whole Foods and Dean & DeLuca (those impersonal grocery hawks that have landed on his turf!) are making him more irrelevant every day? What has kept him from going sour, as so many others would have in his shoes?

We would perhaps all agree that happiness is more about *being* than about *having;* we might say it's about the heart resting in the right place. We know too that there's more to being happy than the mere rejection of its many impostors, such as materialism or hedonism. The path to happiness is quite mysterious. It is found by some and it completely escapes other very good people. This is problematic. If God exists and wants happiness for all of us, there must be good reason why his design, or formula, seems to fail so frequently.

That underlining doubt about whether God is capable of intervening in our lives for the good is the engine of the self-help industry, and also at the heart of its failure. If we begin with the premise that God cannot make a real difference in our lives, it only makes sense to try to work things out all on our own, and to try again and again when our attempts come up short. In bookstores, on television, and on the Internet we find thousands of formulas for self-improvement; sadly, the one thing most of them have in common is a choice to leave God mostly out of the equation for our inner healing. Do phrases like these sound familiar?

- You are the master of your own destiny.

- The center of the universe is *you.*

- Fulfillment is yours without the restraints of imposed tradition.

- You are your own joy.

- If freedom is good, the more freedom the better, and of course freedom from myths of demanding divinities is best.

Since I am not putting these statements—quotes from actual self-help authors—in full context, out of fairness to the authors I will not mention their names. But I'm sure you have read similar pearls of agnostic "wisdom" that profess faith in humanity's complete self-reliance.

One of the problems with the many variations of such atheistic or areligious self-help is this: it doesn't usually work, and it *never* works long-term. These formulas for happiness can help in the short-term by inspiring us to take personal responsibility for practical aspects of our lives, but they can't get us what we yearn for. Authentic happiness is unearthed first by discovering who we are within a universe whose existence is explicable only by the existence of an eternal Creator; happiness is then cultivated as we build a relationship with that Creator, as his son or daughter loved dearly by him.

This discovery and acknowledgment of the Creator-God, and this relationship-building with God our Father, require hard work that nobody can do for us—work that we can call self-help. But if we depend solely on our own strength and wisdom to achieve authentic happiness, as most self-help suggests, we will ultimately be disappointed.

We were created by God out of love. He gave us freedom in order that we might choose what's best for us, to live in friendship with him in this life and for all eternity. Genuine human flourishing, then, almost always has something to do with our good choices (positive self-help) and always has everything to do with God's grace (God-help). Any effort to divorce one from the other is a dangerous detour into philosophical narcissism (pursuing self-help without recognition of God) or religious irrationalism (expecting God to do what he wants us to do for ourselves).

While God doesn't always answer my prayers according to my preferred timing or according to how I think he should, my trust in his promise of real solutions to our troubles is absolute. I know with as much moral certainty as I know anything that God is waiting for you and me to claim the happiness he is holding out to us right now.

Scripture holds a clue as to how we can claim this happiness: "Enter by the narrow gate, since the road that leads to destruction is wide and spacious, and many take it; but it is a narrow gate and a hard road that leads to life, and only a few find it" (Matt. 7:13–14, NJB).

Leave aside for a moment your inclination to read this passage about moral living as a shot across the bow from Jesus to get us to behave better. Leave behind your inclination to see this as a divine guilt trip, a warning to behave well lest you find yourself too far down the "wide and spacious road" of immorality. Think about it instead as Jesus's invitation to go down a wonderful road that leads to *life*. Doesn't this put Christian living into an eminently positive light? Jesus invites us to take the road less traveled because it is the road of life in abundance.

People my parents' and grandparents' age often recall—some nostalgically and most resentfully—how old-time preachers would, with all good intention I'm sure, try to scare them into heaven with apocalyptic depictions of hell. A good Christian must avoid immoral behavior, they were told, in order to escape eternal flames.

Something about that approach doesn't move me, even if it is essentially true: it is foreign to my experience of God's dealings with me and others. Fear-induced morality rarely holds up against the pounding tide of our passions, because we're naturally inclined to satisfy our passions even when our mind tells us there's a better way. And even if we were to live righteous lives out of fear of hell or God's wrath, fear-induced morality results in a lifestyle of rigidity and frustration. Fearful righteousness is far removed from the flourishing, happy, free life God wants for us.

The Bible is essentially a love story between God and us, his sons and daughters. When you read the Gospels—Matthew, Mark, Luke, and John—try to keep your heart wide open to God's whispers. Like an automatic camera lens, whose aperture and shutter speed vary according to the amount of light in the surroundings, our heart is usually partially closed as a type of self-protective mechanism, or it opens and shuts quickly so that only a little light can get in. If we don't fight back against the noise and busyness that surround us, as well as against our preconceived notions (and fear) about what God might want to tell us through the Gospels, our heart will be unable to discern God's quiet, powerful, and eminently respectful voice leading us down a path of fulfillment. When we read scripture, there is no need for fear of too much light. All that light is good for us; our mind and heart need every bit of what God wants to tell us about who he is, who we are, and the great plan that awaits us.

Nowhere is an underdeveloped image of God's will more debilitating and depressing than in the recesses of our soul, where we reflect, with a heart partly closed, on life's big questions regarding our own sinfulness, the "why" of our suffering, the possibility of redemption, our "mission" in life, and the afterlife. Such an underdeveloped image usually speaks to us only of guilt, fear, and shame, and it darkens our outlook on how good life can be right now, no matter what our past or present looks like, and on how accessible happiness and heaven are for all of us.

A mostly open heart, on the other hand, will always be filled with rays of light and joy as it confronts Jesus's approach to these big questions. Before you read the next few pages, take a moment to open your heart. Tell Jesus you aren't afraid of his loving light ready to shine in and illuminate your life with his truth.

You may remember the following story from the Gospel of Mark (10:17–30, NRSV):

Jesus is just about to set out on a journey when a man runs up to him and kneels down. We don't know much about the man, but the fact that the Gospel writer notes he was *running* and then suddenly *knelt down before* Jesus indicates that he was probably a young guy. Later we find out that he was wealthy, and rather liked being wealthy, so we can add to our picture that he was probably dressed up pretty nicely, but pious and eager enough not to worry about getting his nice suit dirty as he fell to the ground in homage.

We get an even better image of this rich young man from the dialogue that follows. As soon as he hits his knees, he blurts out a question to Jesus in a respectful but earnest tone: "Good Teacher, what must I do to inherit eternal life?" After testing the young man's faith by asking him why he had called him "good" if only God is good—he did this so that the young man would recognize that his faith in Jesus was already very deep—Jesus responded to the question about earning salvation by saying, "You know the commandments," and then listing a very demanding set of moral standards (some of the Ten Commandments).

Most people would have gotten up and walked away at this point. But not this rich, pious young man! "Teacher, I have kept all these since my youth," he responded indignantly. And maybe he had, at least in his own mind. How else would he have had the chutzpah to look into the eyes of God and make such a claim! Mark, the evangelist, then reports that Jesus, "looking at him, loved him and said, 'You lack one thing; go, sell what you own, and give the money to the poor, and you will have treasure in heaven; then come, follow me.'"

Having heard Jesus's warning to this moral-minded young man, the disciples asked with obvious concern in their voice, "Then who can be saved?" They were worried for themselves—not just for where they would spend their eternity (heaven or hell), but also for making some sense of their present, for knowing their purpose in life, what they had to look forward to, whether following the teachings of this itinerant preacher would offer them some answers about all the discord, pain, war, and selfishness involved in the human condition. They were hoping that Jesus's teachings would improve their quality of life, and yet now he seemed so harsh.

After all, they had thrown in their lot with Jesus of Nazareth— with his being who he said he was, a friend and brother, Lord and Redeemer. They had altered their life priorities to coincide with his message of love, service, and forgiveness as the solution to humanity's very checkered record. They had begun to fall in love with a God of love who had loved them first by creating them; and who, in the person of Jesus, was loving them as nobody had loved them before.

But now their good master seemed to be saying that some very good people weren't good enough for him. It seemed he was hanging the rich young man out to dry, just because the guy was unwilling to sell all that he had in order to give it to the poor. Maybe they weren't rich like that man, but surely these rough men of the sea didn't consider themselves any holier than he was. Was Jesus going to be just another chapter in the story of God asking of us the impossible?

Maybe it was in this vein that Moe, the butcher, exclaimed to me, "Don't I wish!" when hearing my proposition that he was on his way to becoming another saint. He was speaking for many of us who, though happy, live in differing degrees of fear and doubt over our odds of making the final cut. We muse, "If the Bible is true and heaven is full of saints, then I'm in deep trouble, because alongside those saints I will be terribly out of place." As life rolls on and becomes increasingly complicated, often with more regrets than victories emblazoned on our memory, it is so easy to throw in the towel on our chances of ever acquiring deep happiness.

That's why Jesus's answer to the disciples' question about who can be saved is such fabulous news. It is our reason for hope. It is our key to happiness here and now. It is what gives us peace, even as we look at our own weakness and inadequacy as followers of Jesus. It is what gives me confidence that Moe—and you and I—can someday join the ranks of saints in heaven, notwithstanding our inglorious past or deeply flawed present.

Jesus turned to them, and said, "For mortals it is impossible, but not for God; for God all things are possible."

ALL THINGS ARE possible. Life in abundance. In other words, there is real hope for all of us. If we are willing to accept and collaborate with God's desire and power to save us from our own self-destructive devices, no matter our past, he will help us become flourishing, happy, spirit-filled people. Jesus's final response clarifies that he didn't have it in for the rich, or any other class of people. He just knew that in the case of *this* rich man, the *attachment* to his riches was tearing him down, eating him up, and limiting his potential for personal fulfillment and redemption. Mark says in his Gospel, as we saw earlier, "Jesus, looking at him, loved him and said, 'You lack one thing . . .'"

With hearts fully open, we can read in this biblical story that Jesus was concerned about what good thing was lacking in this man's life. And he wanted *that* for him! That's good news for us: most of us are attached to things or attitudes or beliefs that keep us lacking one or many good things God wants for us.

As I got to know Moe a bit better, I found out that his broad smile was interconnected with the generosity of another man in the neighborhood. Moe explained to me one day, after refusing to let me pay for yet another half pound of ground beef, that the only reason he'd been able to stay in business, even as his swath of "Little Italy" had undergone gentrification and morphed into the über-trendy Nolita (or "north of Little Italy") district, is that the owner of the wildly popular Café Habana restaurant, just down the street from Moe's butcher shop, had chosen (at a significant cost to the restaurant's bottom line) to buy all of his meat from Moe's little shop.

How would Moe have dealt with going out of business? Probably pretty well, because I know now that Moe is not dependent on circumstances for his overall happiness. Still, I'm quite confident that this restaurant owner's generosity was part of God's promise to Moe to bring forth a greater good out of tough situations like this, if Moe let him. Even if Moe would never admit it himself, he let God take over, and God did not let him down.

I wonder what the back story is of the Habana owner's charity to Moe. I'll find out one day, I suspect. My guess would be that somewhere down the line he too had experienced God's love for him through someone else's selfless love. Have you noticed that our goodness spawns goodness in others?

Our goodness has another (more important) effect too—it opens up the human heart to experience God's loving presence. It is next to impossible to experience the personal love of God if one has never experienced the selfless goodness of a neighbor. The more we sow love upon everyone we meet, the better we prepare them for encountering

God's personal, intimate, and unfailing love for them. This experience of God's love launches us into another dimension of our humanity; it is the gate to human flourishing.

Examples like these of good people—*very* good people—who have passed through the narrow gate that brings humanity to life in abundance remind us that following Jesus's road is not an esoteric exercise in positive thinking. It is about how our love relationship with God translates into holy dealings with our husband or wife, bank accounts (yes, bank accounts!), bills, employees, sickness, success, fame, and bad moods.

The message of this book is that human flourishing and beatitude—by that I mean supernatural happiness found through union with God—and finally paradise (heaven) can begin here and now if we become spirit-filled people. We will experience in these pages that heaven is wonderfully accessible to every human being with the courage to turn over the reins of his or her fractured life to a higher and all-loving power. I hope that you will use this book as a guidebook to help you live with enduring confidence and joy, no matter what life brings your way, because we have trusted—indeed, we have come to know— that God looks at us, loves us, and will be faithful to his promises. It is a playbook, if you will, for forging a happy life, a joy-filled life; it suggests ways that, by living consciously and fully the tattered moment of now, we can employ the natural mechanisms of self-improvement God has already forged within us. These, when activated, will open our mind and heart to God's transformative power. In short, in this book I want to share with you how to live now as happy, spirit-filled, heaven-bound saints-in-the-making.

Unlike some self-help books you and I have read before, in these pages I will not promise you the moon. In my estimation, there are no simple secrets that, once revealed and understood by enlightened souls, can attain for you the fulfillment of all your human aspirations. That's because *alone* we cannot control our own future. Sometimes we can't even control the basic well-being of our nearest and dearest—we can't always save our marriage, or get rich through hard work, or be healed when sick. There are too many factors outside of our control. And ironically, many people who *do* succeed at controlling most of these things according to their own idea of bliss end up horribly unsatisfied.

I have said that self-help without God's help is a dangerous life detour. But if we insert self-help into a proper, spiritual understanding of who we are, who God is, and what life is all about, it can prepare us for God's grace. I often read self-help books myself. Taken as a whole, they offer a fascinating case study of where we are as a culture in the ageless pursuit of self-improvement and happiness. I also find in some of them nuggets of true wisdom that catch me by surprise and challenge my ways of thinking. If we can speak of the genius of self-help literature, it is the wonderfully simple truth that God helps those who help themselves. He helps everyone else too, for which we can be thankful—but self-help literature motivates us to embrace our part of his plan for us, to step up to the plate and swing the bat when it's our turn in the batting order. Self-help negates the false spirituality of sitting back and waiting for someone else (God or others) to pinch-hit for us.

While I do sometimes read self-help books, I cringe when I see someone else reading one on the subway or beside me on a plane. I cringe because I know that the person behind those pages is seeking something far greater than what self-help offers, and the author is most likely telling that person that he or she can find it all right there.

As I began to explain earlier in this chapter, the great downfall of the self-help genre is the glorification of human potential, independent of our dependence on God. Logically, self-help without God's help is at best a fleeting solution, for if it works at all, it works only for a finite number of years. Think of this: self-help wasn't responsible for our arrival on this earth, and it has never made anyone live forever.

Let me take this one step further. The fact that our origin and eternal destiny cannot be manipulated by human effort should lead us to question whether self-help *alone* is sufficient even for achieving our full potential here and now. The answer, I believe, is no. For there is nothing I can tell you and there is nothing you can do that by its own merit will meet all of your needs. Your heart is too big to be satisfied by self-help or human help of any kind. You have been made in the image and likeness of God, and your soul will be restless until it rests in him and his plan for you.

Part of that plan, however, is precisely self-help *as a starting gate into the supernatural world.* Self-help is the natural companion of grace. For this reason, with this book I am going to point you down a path of collaboration with the power of God. I am going to show you where self-help is necessary, and where God's help begins. I am confident that if you take this path, freely and conscientiously, it will bring you great fulfillment and inner peace, a peace that has its origin in God and goes way beyond self-manipulated sensory contentment and human understanding. It is a state of soul in which we are profoundly happy with who we are, why we are here, and where we are going, even if much of our human suffering remains.

I am not offering you in these pages a set of good or wise ideas of my own. Instead, I am proposing a renewed lifestyle in accordance with what God has revealed about himself and about us. I am inviting you into a spiritual program that begins whenever you want it to and that will last a lifetime. It will be a challenge and a joy, hard work and utter delight. As we feel the gentle call of the Holy Spirit to set aside our self-destructive habits, we will feel simultaneously the pinch of sacrifice and the overwhelming presence of a loving God who wants to meet us more than halfway.

This integrated, human/supernatural approach to self-improvement is not esoteric. It is not distant. It is not heady. It is not only for philosophers or for the enlightened. It is as down-to-earth as God-Made-Man—in other words, it is as earthy, gritty, and fantastically mundane as Jesus being born in a stable. It is as shockingly human as the Son of God choosing to work in a carpenter's shop for many long years. Our program of life involves tapping into and imitating how Jesus lived his routine. With what conviction and persuasiveness must he have done his simple duties! With what love and thoughtfulness must he have treated his mother and stepfather, his neighbors and friends! What positive and wonderful things must have been on his mind and running through his heart!

Jesus could have come to us riding on a cloud and supported by legions of angels. Instead, he lived like us, he suffered like us, he dealt with imperfect people like us, and all the while he was moving toward fulfilling a mission he had received from his Father. We too have a mission. *You* have a mission. Our spiritual program entails discovering our divine mission in the simplicity and complexity of our present reality.

There's no reason on earth or in heaven that you and I, made in God's image, can't live like Jesus lived. God wants this great gift for us, and he wants us to seek it out.

The other day I spoke to a woman with a very understandable complaint against God: "I'm not asking him for happiness," she said, "for at this point I don't even know what that would be like. All I ask for is a little peace." That peace—and yes, deep and profound happiness too—is within our reach. God is waiting for us to claim those good things along a path only we can tread.

In history, there surely have been many valid variations of the path I want to show you. My desk and bookshelves are filled with writings by spiritual leaders whom I respect, but whose religious and personal backgrounds are far different than my own. They have come to conclusions that sometimes agree with mine and other times contradict them. That's life. God made us a motley crew with tiny brains and broken hearts. I don't believe that you have to be signed up in my parish register to get to heaven (although I hope it helps those who are!). In fact, I'm sure there are today Hindus in India and Jews in Israel who will, by God's grace, be counted among the saints in heaven, and may very well receive a greater reward than I will for their pursuit and acceptance of him in the vestiges of truth, beauty, and goodness that God revealed to them in this life.

That said, I would be dishonest if I were to claim that the many variations of this path to human flourishing and salvation are equally straight and efficient. As a Christian, I take Jesus at his word when he proclaims, "I am the way, and the truth, and the life. No one comes to the Father except through me" (John 14:6, NRSV). I firmly believe that it is through the life, death, and resurrection of Jesus that all men and women, of all times and places, have access to heaven, where every tear shall be wiped away (Rev. 21:4) and where we will become like him, no longer saints-in-the-making, as we can be today, but triumphant members of the communion of the saints.

As simple, and perhaps dogmatic, as that all sounds, I don't fool myself into thinking that one act of belief in Jesus Christ as my Lord and Savior, or many years in his service, makes me a living saint, or even a happy person. I know many miserable Christians. At times in my own life I've felt pretty miserable, in fact. And I must say, I have encountered very sad committed Christians, and even leaders of Christians—priests and pastors—who are frustrated with God for his apparent failure to come through on his end of the bargain, as they understand it.

But isn't this path of the saints that I'm proposing supposed to be about human flourishing, about becoming spirit-filled? If Jesus is the way, and the truth, and the life, and you're following him, why aren't you happy, or why are you only partially happy? What kind of twisted God would lead you to confusion, depression, and pain, or leave you otherwise unsatisfied? Where is the silver lining in trying to be a good person when it seems the wicked have all the fun?

Those are questions that need answers. If this book gives you many nice ideas about God and things spiritual, but doesn't help you become a happier person—a mother, son, spouse, employee, and friend who smiles more often and more effortlessly, who is nicer to be with, who needs fewer crutches to keep standing—this book will have failed. Yes, God made us to flourish, and if we aren't there yet, there must be a way forward.

Throughout this book I will invite you to go from self-help to God's help, then from God's help back to self-help. I will invite you to open yourself to brand new possibilities for altering the way you live in the present, first through the human power of the mind, heart, and will. Sometimes my advice may sound more practical than spiritual. It may, indeed, sound similar to some secular approaches to self-improvement that you may once have dismissed as un-Christian. In other parts of this book you may be equally surprised at how much I ask you to depend on the power of God to transform your life.

My methodology is based on what I consider an integral approach to human development. God made us psychosomatic beings—that is, we have bodies, minds, and souls, and each affects the others. While we are powerless to save ourselves or even to be completely happy through our own strength, God is waiting for us to activate the powers of our body and psychology, of our mind and will, as part of our growth process. He expects us to get all of this in shape so that our soul, in turn, will be ready for the transformative work of his grace.

This human preparation, self-help, is hard work, and it must be done artistically. It involves forming new and positive thought and behavior patterns that will take the place of the self-destructive patterns we have become accustomed to, and that stand in the way of our becoming everything God created us to be. Learning to get out of God's way, then, and letting him help us, is equally artistic.

I have divided our adventure into three sections. The first is titled "The Problem." It explains why we get stuck in our pursuit of happiness and sets forth principles for what we can do about it. The second section is titled "The Faith-Hope-Love Cure." It explains God's plan for bringing us to personal fulfillment. The third section is titled "The Program." It is meant to inspire us along our daily journey of transformation as we move to and from self-help and God's help.

If you want to make this adventure, I invite you to join me.

PART I

The Problem

CHAPTER I

Junior Partners of the Holy Spirit

As we begin our journey, I want to recall a simple spiritual truth: God has chosen to need us in the project of our redemption. Some theologians may dispute the linguistic convenience of such a bold statement, but I'm confident that it not only is true, but is one of the keys to understanding God's way of dealing with us. God has ordered the world in such a way that even his greatest miracles don't usually happen without human collaboration. The Bible didn't drop down from the clouds; it was passed down in oral and written form by people who could have gone home instead and lain down on the couch. Babies don't show up at our door; a man and woman come together and become cocreators with God. The Good Samaritan who went out of his way to console his downtrodden neighbor was Jesus's preferred social justice strategy—an individual taking personal responsibility to do the right thing. And then, finally, there's God's choice to attach salvation to our faith, that mysteriously free, simple, complicated, misty gift from God by which we are saved.

God's many blessings to us are truly his, for he is their origin and he sustains us, but most of his blessings are delivered, or left behind, undelivered, by ordinary people like you and me. He has tied the expression of his love to our free will.

Deeply accepting our irreplaceable role in becoming everything God created us to be already places us way ahead of the curve. The emotional shackles of helplessness and uselessness that confine so many people in mediocrity and the status quo slowly loosen and will eventually disappear if we act in accordance with this truth. Deeply accepting that our progress depends neither upon others, nor upon variable circumstances, is a tipping point from stagnation to growth. This deep acceptance is not a mind game. It is a spiritual conviction, accepted by the intellect, that God wants me to be free from my self-limiting patterns. It implies deeply accepting that God is waiting for me to *do* something, to use the natural mechanisms of mind and will to claim my own freedom!

In the project of personal renewal, we can't wait for the perfect time, or for some irresistible inspiration, or for a spectacular convergence of events. We must just *begin*. Spiritual procrastination is the art of coming up with more or less convincing reasons why we can't do now what we know God would want us to do. It is the sordid art of justifying to ourselves why we shouldn't commit ourselves fully to what God surely or probably wills for us.

Our excuses for inaction often convince us, because we know that even if we were ready to change our lives, we wouldn't know exactly how to do it, or whether we would fail along the way. In the chapters to come, we will learn how to replace negative thought and behavior patterns with positive ones in real-life situations, but none of that technique will work long-term if our action is not of a certain kind.

Effective action toward self-improvement is what we can call *Junior Partner* action. Junior Partners in the business world have real responsibility, represent the company in front of clients, do the heavy lifting on projects, and share in the profits, but in the end they are not the company. Someone above them—the Senior Partner—is backing them up, is in ultimate control, and makes sure the right things happen.

Our work relationship with the Holy Spirit, our collaboration with God, is not unlike that model. Without God's inspiration, the authors of scripture, even had they stayed off the couch, would have written just another reference book. Even the proudest of parents know that the product of their sexual union—their child's uniqueness and spiritual soul—far exceeds their own creative powers. And what or who moved the heart of the Good Samaritan that Jesus spoke of in the Gospel to recognize real suffering in another and come to the aid of his neighbor in such a remarkable way, going far beyond the call of duty? The Holy Spirit is living and active and is waiting for us to join his team! In other words, behind the scenes of our efforts to live our destiny of becoming spirit-filled people is an all-loving, all-powerful, personal, and providential God who is ready to work with us. He will meet us halfway, three-quarters of the way, or even almost all the way—as far as we need him to go.

Working as Junior Partners of the Holy Spirit requires a lot of humility. A humble spiritual Junior Partner is conscious of his weakness, and yet perfectly confident in the presence, wisdom, and strength of his Boss. As St. Paul said, "So, I will boast all the more gladly of my weaknesses, so that the power of Christ may dwell in me" (2 Cor. 12:9, NRSV).

Forging such humility is in great part a work of learning to be attentive to the action of the Holy Spirit in our lives. Just as a truly humble spouse is attentive to the needs and sensitivities of the one he loves, we can become more effective Junior Partners by greater attentiveness to what the Holy Spirit is up to in our lives and in the world. We can form the habit of conversing with God throughout the day even about the most ordinary of events. This is done in the form of simple prayers of thanksgiving (for example, "Thank you, God, for giving me the words to say in that situation"), of petition (for example, "Jesus, help me to keep my peace in this meeting"), or of praise (for example, "God, I love you and want to live my life for you"). When regular contact with God through prayer becomes a constant throughout our day, we are more apt to hear his whispers. They usually come in the form of fresh ideas or intuitions, calls to our conscience to rectify our attitudes or behavior, silent invitations to say something kind or carry out some good work for someone else, or spiritual consolation (the abatement of anxiety, new inner peace, and so on).

Humble attentiveness to God's action around us brings great peace. Junior Partners of the Holy Spirit are profoundly peaceful people. They are at once confident in God's loving and active presence in their endeavors and also fully engaged in carrying out his will. Getting to this point of serene abandonment and commitment to God's will can either happen gracefully, as in the case of gradual and continuous spiritual growth, or with great pains, as in the case of someone who hits rock bottom in her personal life and finally turns her life over to God as a last resort.

Not long ago I got an anonymous message informing me that a friend of mine, Dave, had been admitted to the hospital for "exhaustion," adding that everything was fine and he would be released in a few days. I knew that Dave had been under quite a bit of professional stress, because he was in the midst of a significant corporate acquisition, but I also knew him to be a take-charge kind of guy who was able to juggle with admirable aplomb his many family and professional duties. The "exhaustion" explanation seemed improbable. And so it was. For the next twenty-four hours I tried with no success to reach Dave. The hospital wouldn't give me his room number, and Dave wasn't answering his cell phone. Eventually, he called from an "unknown number"—so my phone announced—and apologized for the disappearing act. From the sound of his voice I could tell that something significant was afoot. I would have expected him to assure me immediately that everything was fine. He didn't. With no excuses and in a humble tone, Dave informed me that his family had admitted him to a drug and alcohol rehabilitation program. I would never have guessed in a million years that this straitlaced, got-it-together guy had serious addictions. I knew him well and had never knowingly seen him drunk or otherwise under the influence of drugs. In fact, he was a very pious man who was deeply involved with and committed to his Presbyterian church in South Florida.

While I'm sure Dave could have used his intelligence and charm to play along with the game of rehabilitation and get back quickly to his old ways, I knew that he was serious about reform when the first thing he did was turn over the reins of his business to his business partner. Under guidance from his doctors, he agreed not to set any mental deadlines for recovery, and he was brutally honest with his family about the origin and extent of his problem. He revealed that he had been drinking to get drunk several times a week for several years. Business travel had been his cover. But in the last few months, with business pressures building closer to home, relatives and friends noticed he had begun to put on a lot of weight and always wanted to be alone at night. Eventually, Dave explained, his craving for alcohol and "daytime substances" took control of his life. He had feared that sooner or later his well-crafted façade would crumble, and now, much sooner than expected, his ability to manage the mess was gone.

It's hard to determine what combination of virtues and fortune gives a guy like Dave the courage to tackle his problem with so much honesty and persistence the first time. I've seen many people in worse situations than his (facing terrible self-image issues, an abusive relationship, pornography or sex addiction, out-of-control spending, infidelity, depression, an eating disorder) spend a precious lifetime denying their problems, blaming others, and generally resisting reform. Many factors come into play, of course, that have an effect on our decisions, for the story of human liberty is as complex as the human race is diverse; but Dave's story of a good beginning to what has turned out to be a great success story has one quality that I find present in every genuinely successful comeback—it is the quality of spiritual humility.

Junior Partners of the Holy Spirit are essentially humble people who prepare their souls to be touched and transformed by grace. They are men and women who have come to recognize that there is a higher power, that they are not it, and that they need it. Humble people who are then touched by grace experience this higher power as a personal and loving Father/Mother who invites them to be part of his/her great plan for their happiness. We mustn't confuse spiritual humility with being a pious pushover. The bulldozer Type-A personality that Dave is, for example, doesn't have to give up who he is when faced with his own weakness and God's love. He simply becomes the unique Junior Partner he was created to be, doing things only Junior Partners of his personality type and personal history can do.

Giving over the reins of our life to God doesn't mean sitting back and watching life go by. True abandonment of ourselves to God's will is not a passive approach to living; instead it involves a commitment to developing our talents and personality to their maximum potential, because God has chosen to need us in reaching out to others. In our diversity of personality traits and skills and passions, as Junior Partners we come together to form a beautiful quilt that reflects God's perfect being.

Dave's process of becoming a Junior Partner of the Holy Spirit was quite remarkable for the depth and speed of his spiritual renewal. After his initial and sincere acceptance of his problem, Dave dedicated himself to several months of professional treatment. But he immediately realized that his problem was not just psychological or physical. Dave saw that he had some major work to do in his personal life and realized that it would need to begin with a review of his relationship with God. He understood that he needed to get at the root of what propelled him to overdrink. Dave asked me for some regular spiritual guidance, and since I was in New York and he was in Florida, I told him he should look for someone who could guide him more closely. Nevertheless, I sent him an outline that he could use as a starting point for his journey of spiritual growth. It included questions to help him identify his main character weakness and then figure out the virtue that would lead him in spiritual growth.

Below is a summary of the analysis and plan Dave came up with. I'm including it here as a concrete example of someone who took seriously his role as Junior Partner. I don't recommend copying what he has done, for everyone has his or her own journey to make, but the honest and humble introspection and commitment that Dave worked on is imitable, for sure, and can be a launching pad for anyone's spiritual growth. (Dave used the outline I offer in my book *The Promise: God's Purpose and Plan for When Life Hurts* as his guide.)

Sketching a Plan for My Spiritual Life:
Dave's Version

1. What would you say is the major obstacle to your spiritual progress? You can call this your "root sin." The three major root sins, as identified by some of the great spiritual teachers, are pride (egotism), vanity, and sensuality (inordinate love of pleasure).

My root sin is vanity. Reading the description of vanity in your book *The Promise* was both startling and humbling, because I didn't believe that I was a vain person. But I do enjoy pleasing people. My concern with physical appearance comes and goes, but it is definitely present. I am driven by success and interpret my own self-worth by whether or not I'm successful. My fear of failing causes me to put off making certain decisions or engaging in activities that may fail, knowing that failure would shame me. At other times I lie to avoid getting into trouble. I want to be popular, although I always said that popularity wasn't important to me. But it is—I'm just afraid that I wouldn't be popular if I said it. I crave success—visualize it, dream about it—but the slightest failure discourages me and sets me back emotionally and spiritually.

2. How does your root sin—in this case, vanity—manifest itself in your daily life?

I'm always joking around so folks will laugh and be drawn to me. Some of this I learned in my childhood as a way of getting people to like me.

I get depressed, upset, and angry when my business plans for success don't pan out or when they prove more difficult to achieve than I expected. I often just drop whatever I am working on and move on.

I routinely shade the truth so as to not "make people feel bad" or so that I look better than what actually happened. I also sometimes refrain from speaking up so as to not cause people to not like me.

3. What spiritual goal is God calling you to work toward to counter your root sin? You can call this your "opposite virtue." Some examples of opposite virtues for the root sins are as follows: for pride—humility, attitude of service, patience, forgiveness, kindness, obedience to God, generosity, constant concern for others, charity; for vanity—humility, honesty, principled decision-making, love of God above all things, charity; for sensuality— tenacity, attitude of service, self-control, purity in our thoughts and actions, moderation, self-sacrifice.

I think I should take "humility" as the opposite virtue to overcome my vanity. This will mean being honest even when the truth makes me look bad, making principled decisions, loving other people for who they are even when it doesn't feel good, giving priority to my prayer life (or starting one) and going to church every Sunday, and living for others and not myself, especially those I am closest to, starting with my wife and family.

4. What threats do you see that might hinder you from obtaining this goal, in your relationship with God, with others, and in your interior life or self-discipline?

I think that the threats to obtaining my spiritual goal are these:

In my relationship with God:

- I do not pray every morning, at night, or during the day. God is not a living part of my life.

- I take God's love and grace for granted and focus on what people give me.

- I act without thinking or considering God's plan and design for me, thus abusing my body, my mind, my heart, and my spirituality.

In my relationships with others:

- I let things that I disagree with or that I feel are untrue, or hurtful, or wrong go unchallenged—I "swallow" them—mostly out of fear of confrontation and fear that I won't be liked. Consequently, these "slights" build up and eventually get the better of me.

- I joke too much, even in serious situations, without using the judgment to stop and offer some other form of support or charity to the people with whom I am dealing.

- I flirt with women too often, and although nothing improper has occurred, I know that such behaviors are not supportive of my wife and are not the best, most fulfilling and spiritual relationships that I can have with others.

In my interior life (self-discipline):

- I brood over problems, over personal slights, over failure of employees to follow my directions. I let these problems build up and get too big.

- I waste time dreaming of success rather than working out the tiny details necessary for success.

- I dream up different avenues or scenarios by which I would be popular or people would like me.

5. What strategy can you design to address these threats and move toward achieving your spiritual goal?

Here is what I have decided to do to become a better Junior Partner of the Holy Spirit as I work toward the spiritual goal that I know God is inviting me to:

In my relationship with God:

- I will use the little prayer book a friend from work gave to me. Before my day starts or ends, I will pray from that book. I will read a psalm daily, along with the biblical prayer of Elizabeth as she greeted Jesus's mother. These will make me think about God and will enhance my relationship with him.

- When working on projects, I will pause, thank God for his mercy, and ask for strength.

- In addition to church attendance, I will devote Sunday mornings to reading the Bible and other holy works.

In my relationships with others:

- I will no longer exaggerate my personal victories or successes. I will no longer go along with the statements of others out of fear, but will speak up in a respectful way when the occasion deserves it.

- I will use better judgment as to when joking is appropriate, and I will look for ways to offer compliments, make positive comments, and offer support to others.

- I will strive to give those closest to me my time and support, beginning with my wife and family.

In my interior life (self-discipline):

- I will spend "mind time"—the time I typically spend dreaming—praying instead, meditating on the words of Jesus, and learning to take his message to heart.

- Whenever I start to become tempted by vanity or to act in a vain manner, I will purify my thoughts: I will stop what I am doing, think of God, and think of his design for me.

- I will share my thoughts and my struggles with those closest to me and not pretend that I am doing something that I am not.

Perhaps you were struck with how specific and practical Dave's spiritual plan is—it's like a business plan for the soul. As noted earlier, he followed an outline for spiritual progress presented in my first book, *The Promise*. This pragmatic approach works well for some and not so well for others. But all of us can admire Dave's willingness to recognize his failings and to offer to God a mind, heart, and body ready for his grace.

Dave has stuck with the promises he made to God and himself. The road has not been easy, and he would never say that he's made it. But his inner healing has been as real as his recovery from addiction. He has experienced God's grace in powerful ways, and above all he is working on his spiritual growth every day.

Below is a poem Dave penned to God and sent to me from his hospital room. It reveals another face of the same spiritual humility:

Where have you been all my life?
Where have you been?
You were there beside me all along.
I found you once, but then forgot.
You were with me all along.
I didn't say much to you,
I never said I love you.
I dishonored you and cursed you.
But you were there all along.
You saw my pain.
You felt my confusion.
You wept for me.
All along, you never flinched, you never left,
You were there for me.
You always have been.
You always will be.

I love you, Jesus,
I love you.

By gradual and continual spiritual growth (the most painless way), or by hitting rock bottom and turning to God (Dave's way), or by gnawing one's way to the top of worldly success and finding out that happiness isn't there (think some business executives or Hollywood celebrities), the spiritually humble find themselves adjusting their behavior and attitudes to the ways of God, whom they come to know as a loving and forgiving Father who is on their side.

I invite you to begin your Junior Partnership with the Holy Spirit, even now as you move through the attitudes God wants us to have as we approach God's plan for our happiness. First, ask God to give you a deep acceptance, as I have suggested, of your role in becoming the spirit-filled person he has always meant you to be. Then listen to the whispers of the Holy Spirit in these pages as he invites you to leave behind patterns of self-limiting thought and behavior and replace them with new thought patterns and a lifestyle of the living saints, who are the happiest people in the world.

CHAPTER 2

Making Straight the Path

When I think of John the Baptist, I think of a bearded guy dressed in hairy garments, eating grasshoppers in the desert, and calling out like a madman things nobody wanted to hear: "Repent!" "Make way for the Lord." "Make straight the path!" Admittedly, the image I've had most of my life of Jesus's cousin John is rather uninspiring. It's also rather incomplete, for he must have had fabulously compelling qualities too. We know that people flocked to him—and when they did they were moved by him to such an extent that they were "filled with expectation" (Luke 3:15, NAB). John did everything in his power to warn people that he wasn't the one they were looking for. He went as far as saying that he was so inferior to the Messiah whose coming he was called by God to predict and prepare that he would be unworthy to untie his sandals!

Maybe it was John's humility that made him such an attractive and credible prophet. People knew he had something special going on, and—Messiah or not—people of every walk of life sought his humble and fearless advice. They wanted to know *what they were supposed to do* to get ready for the Messiah. They wanted to know how to prepare for God's help, which John promised was on its way. And John gave them straight talk:

> The crowds asked [John the Baptist], "What then should we do?" He said to them in reply, "Whoever has two cloaks should share with the person who has none. And whoever has food should do likewise." Even tax collectors came to be baptized and they said to him, "Teacher, what should we do?" He answered them, "Stop collecting more than what is prescribed." Soldiers also asked him, "And what is it that we should do?" He told them, "Do not practice extortion, do not falsely accuse anyone, and be satisfied with your wages." (Luke 3:10–14, NAB)

The Gospel says "*even* tax collectors came." I take this to mean that most people who came to seek John's advice were more like us, less notably public sinners, but a mess all the same: tired moms and dads, frustrated teachers, anxious students, lonely singles, discontent spouses, busy business owners, architects, clergy, and carpenters whose lives were in need of one or another type of reordering. Can't you hear John's raspy voice (he ate grasshoppers, after all) speak simple truth to each of us? To our questions of what we should do, he responds, "Get that part of your life that you know is out of whack back on track. Do what you know you should do, and do it now!"

John didn't explain his commands. He didn't tell the soldiers why they shouldn't practice extortion or accuse people falsely. Nor did he give the tax collectors a course in business ethics. He just told them to stop rationalizing their behavior and to do the right thing. He told them to stop pretending and to be real. He told them to bite the bullet and pay the small price of starting over with the right foot forward.

John was able to be this straightforward and succinct because he knew God had imprinted on each of our souls a basic sense of right and wrong—something philosophers have come to call "natural law." This innate sense of right and wrong is valid for every human being, regardless of cultural or religious upbringing. We don't always know the minutiae of God's will for us, and very often we don't know how to get unstuck from the marsh we've gotten mired in, but if we take time to reflect with the honesty John recommended to his followers, we can know right and wrong in big strokes and at least get our ship pointed in the right direction as we await God's crane of grace to lift us up and out and into calm ports. God wants us to leave behind the marsh and enter into the perfect place (physical, emotional, financial, relational, and spiritual) he has prepared for us. But John knew his cousin Jesus—knew him well enough to know that he would never wave a wand of success and redemption over anyone's unwilling heart. For this reason he warned everyone, continuously and insistently, that they should do *something* to show Jesus they were willing and ready for him to work a miracle on and in them.

Today too, out of a deep and mysterious respect for our free will, Jesus awaits a sign from us that we want his help. From what I've witnessed, in my life and in others' lives, almost any sincere sign will do— pick up a Bible and ask God for inspiration, raise up a heartfelt prayer of petition for God's help, or simply ask God for the gift of faith.

John the Baptist was a big proponent of self-help, as we have seen, but he was just as adamant about pointing to our inability to attain on our own the fullness of God's great plans for us. He baptized people in water as a sign of their repentance from their old ways and of their choosing a new beginning. And curiously, all this time he reminded his followers—the very ones he was baptizing—that what he was doing for them was not enough. It wouldn't save them. It wouldn't bring them eternal life. It wouldn't even satisfy the deepest longings of their heart, the ones they had been searching for aimlessly and unsuccessfully through the pursuit of selfish choices. They needed a Messiah. They needed Jesus.

> John answered them all, saying, "I am baptizing you with water, but one mightier than I is coming. I am not worthy to loosen the thongs of his sandals. He will baptize you with the Holy Spirit and fire. . . . Exhorting them in many other ways, he preached good news to the people. (Luke 3:16–18, NAB)

Why was John promising baptism in the Spirit? What was the good news he was preaching "in many other ways"? Jesus answered that question for us when he said to a good and sincere man named Nicodemus, "Truly, truly, I say to you, unless one is born of water *and the spirit* he cannot see the Kingdom of God." And later, "Do not be amazed that I say to you, 'You must be born again'" (John 3:3, 7, NAB).

Becoming spirit-filled people is, in essence, being baptized in the Spirit of God. It happens through the Divine Cure of faith, hope, and love. Upcoming chapters will outline how this baptism in the spirit can happen to us, how we can open our souls and allow God to do his part in breaking us free from our self-destructive and self-limiting patterns of thought and behavior, how he helps us to become everything he created us to be. But this miracle, this cure, is still dependent on the kind of self-help John the Baptist asked of his disciples. John's self-help plan was rooted in radical honesty about one's past and present reality and a firm conviction to change and make amends with the help of God's grace.

We can extrapolate on John's plan by marking out in six steps what true self-help requires of us. We can call these six steps the Make Straight the Path process, borrowing John's mantra to the world for how to prepare the way for the Lord. These steps represent our preparation for a miracle God is waiting to give us. No matter where we are in life, no matter what is holding us back, these steps are for us. I keep a copy of them on my desk, and I review them and recommit myself to them every day.

Make Straight the Path

1. Make a searching and fearless moral inventory of your life.

2. Admit to God, to yourself, and to other human beings the exact nature of your wrongs and your powerlessness over them.

3. Turn your will over to God's care and live trusting that he can make you whole.

4. Begin to live the so-called New Commandment: "Love one another as I have loved you" (John 15:12, RSV).

5. Make amends to anyone you have harmed along the way with your selfish pursuits.

6. Design and follow a practical plan to hold yourself accountable to God and to others.

42 ❧ GOD WANTS YOU HAPPY

God will accompany us and give us strength to carry through with this work, but he won't do any of these steps for us. If out of fear or shame we look for shortcuts and skip any one of them, the spiritual fruits of faith, hope, and love that God is waiting to give us will be truncated. Our growth in the Spirit of God will be stunted. We may become better people, but we will not be spirit-filled, and our happiness will not be complete.

Those familiar with the teachings of Alcoholics Anonymous will recognize in the above steps a partial reflection of its twelve-step program. Even if we have never struggled with physical addiction, all of us are unhealthily attached to something, or someone, or some series of thoughts or behaviors that limit our spiritual freedom. We are less filled with the Holy Spirit than we could otherwise be because we repeatedly do things and cultivate thoughts that we know, with some honest reflection, are not good for us. Why aren't we able to let these patterns go? And more poignantly for the Christian, we ask, "Why doesn't Jesus make these unseemly things go away when we ask this of him?"

The single prerequisite of being a Junior Partner of the Spirit is a willingness to put our shoulder to the plow and make straight the path for the Lord. Self-improvement starts with a very human process of conversion or repentance from old ways of doing things, all of which prepares us for life in the Spirit.

I didn't know Jim very well, but besides seeing him on most Sundays in the second to the last pew, partially and conveniently hidden from my view and from my sermon behind a big Gothic column, he and I would run into each other at the most unlikely of times and places—on a golf course in another state, at a crosswalk on the Upper East Side of Manhattan, and at a church in Ohio where I was visiting family. Our contact was always cordial, and we joked about having each other's GPS coordinates programmed into our phones.

It was a Saturday afternoon when his e-mail appeared in my iPhone. I didn't recognize the sender's name, but after reading his introductory line—"You may not remember me, but I'm the guy from your church you always run into," I knew exactly who he was. After reading his second line I braced myself for what I figured would be a gut-wrenching story: "I'm writing you because I didn't know who else to turn to."

Jim set up his problem by saying he had been seeing a girl for about six months and had come to love her very much. She loved him too and they had talked about marriage. They were both in their thirties and had dated around for many years, wondering why relationship after relationship just wasn't right. This one was different for both of them: even after such a short time, they couldn't imagine carrying on without the other.

There was just one problem, and it was getting bigger. As Jim described it, "I'm a compulsive liar and Samantha is at her wits' end." Jim explained in that e-mail and then later in person the nature of his lying. Nothing terrible had happened between him and Samantha. He had not been unfaithful to their relationship and she knew all the important things about his past and present, but almost daily Samantha would catch him exaggerating, covering up, or flat out making things up. None of the lies at face value was of much importance, but in the moment of decision, Jim simply couldn't help himself from describing a false, rosier version of reality. His lying was almost automatic, as if a reflex. And while Jim would later give Samantha the real story if she called him out, Samantha saw things from a different angle: the sillier the lie, the worse it was, for it meant Jim was willing to hurt her without any reason at all. It also meant he could not be trusted.

We'll get back to Jim and Samantha's story of eventual self-help and God-help, leading to spiritual freedom, but first let's contrast Jim's attitude toward truth to that of one of my favorite Bible characters:

[Jesus] entered Jericho and was passing through. And there was a man called by the name of Zaccheus; he was a chief tax collector and he was rich. Zaccheus was trying to see who Jesus was, and was unable because of the crowd, for he was small in stature. So he ran on ahead and climbed up into a sycamore tree in order to see him, for he was about to pass through that way. When Jesus came to the place, he looked up and said to him, "Zaccheus, hurry and come down, for today I must stay at your house." And he hurried and came down and received him gladly. When they saw it, they all began to grumble, saying, "He has gone to be the guest of a man who is a sinner." Zaccheus stopped and said to the Lord, "Behold, Lord, half of my possessions I will give to the poor, and if I have defrauded anyone of anything, I will give back four times as much." And Jesus said to him, "Today salvation has come to this house, because he, too, is a son of Abraham. For the Son of Man has come to seek and save that which was lost." (Luke 19:1–10, NASB)

What do we know about Zaccheus? Lots, actually. From every one of the details Luke gives us about him, we can deduce others and paint a good picture of his personality and the state of his heart.

Zaccheus was a chief tax collector and he was rich.

Tax collectors during Roman times were the worst of the worst: they were Jews who would collect money from their own people and give it to the oppressive pagan rulers. *Rich* tax collectors, like Zaccheus, were those who were especially good at collecting more than what was owed. And Zaccheus was not only rich, but he was a *chief* tax collector, meaning he knew how to manage and manipulate other shameless traitors. The man was shrewd and could care less about what his own people thought of him.

> Zaccheus was trying to see who Jesus was, and was unable because of the crowd, for he was small in stature. So he ran on ahead and climbed up into a sycamore tree in order to see him, for he was about to pass through that way.

Everyone in the region had heard of Jesus of Nazareth and the great wonders he was performing. They had also heard his message of being the Messiah, the Son of God, who had come to earth to draw all men and women to repentance and salvation. Knowing all of this, and knowing well the life of sin and questionable morality he had chosen for himself, Zaccheus still wanted to see Jesus—in fact, he wanted it badly enough to run ahead and climb a tree. He didn't care about being mocked for being "short of stature"; he didn't care about being called a spiritual hypocrite or even having someone point him out to Jesus as a sinner. Zaccheus had a sense (an inspiration?) that this man named Jesus was important for him, and he used his shrewd mind to determine Jesus's exact path, "for he was about to pass through that way." Zaccheus had made a decision to do his part.

> When Jesus came to the place, he looked up and said to him, "Zaccheus, hurry and come down, for today I must stay at

your house." And he hurried and came down and received him gladly.

Even as Zaccheus was doing his part to encounter God, we see here how God's grace was at work. Jesus called Zaccheus by name. He didn't call him a tax collector; he didn't call him a thief; he didn't even point out how silly he looked perched in a sycamore tree, with all those gold rings on his fingers and gold chains dangling from his lowered, outstretched neck. He called him *by name.* This was Zaccheus's clue that Jesus knew him inside and out and therefore also knew that Zaccheus's heart was ready. I love how Jesus was in a hurry to take advantage of this open and honest heart: "Hurry and come down, for today I must stay at your house." I picture Zaccheus jumping down awkwardly, short, stubby legs and all, and cupping Jesus's hands in his: "He hurried down and received him gladly," says the Gospel. Most of us, in Zaccheus's shoes, would be concerned about the condition of our bachelor pad. We would want some time to hide the previous night's unjust collection behind the niche in the wall. We would worry about putting on a show, or perhaps getting in a few good jabs at the pious crowds, many of whom would have given much to dine with Jesus. Not Zaccheus. His life was an open book—a dirty book, but an open book. And that's apparently the kind Jesus loves. As the account concludes, "the Son of Man has come to seek and save that which was lost."

When they saw it, they all began to grumble, saying, "He has gone to be the guest of a man who is a sinner."

Despite Jesus's ever-so-obvious lesson of who will be saved—not the perfect, but rather the honest and the willing—Jesus's followers didn't get it. They didn't get it because they didn't know they were sinners! They grumbled, "He has gone to be the guest of a man who is a sinner." Not even the Son of God could work the miracle of being these people's guest, of entering into their lives, of healing them from their woundedness, of giving them the gift of redemption—because in their minds they weren't lost. They loved Jesus as an ornament on their altar of self-worship.

> Zaccheus stopped and said to the Lord, "Behold, Lord, half of my possessions I will give to the poor, and if I have defrauded anyone of anything, I will give back four times as much."

Jesus knew that Zaccheus was the real deal because he reads hearts. We know he was the real deal because we see how he changed his life. In the second chapter of the book of James, we read: "For just as the body without the spirit is dead, so faith without works is also dead" (James 2:26, NRSV). And if Zaccheus's new commitment is a measure of his faith, his faith is fully alive and immense. First he's going to give half of what he has to the poor, and then he's going to repay all the people he's defrauded—and repay them not just once but fourfold. Clearly the man is willing to go into debt, and he'll have to find a new job to boot!

> And Jesus said to him, "Today salvation has come to this house."

Zaccheus's rather expensive commitment to make amends pales in comparison to the value of eternal life Jesus gave to him. It's awesome to consider that Jesus's gift was not given in return for Zaccheus's resolution, nor given under any other condition. There was no quid pro quo, such as we often look for in human relations. Jesus's gift was free, and it's free for anyone with the open and honest heart of Zaccheus, anyone who is willing to give a signal to Jesus that he is a welcomed guest of the soul.

Let's take a look back at the six Make Straight the Path steps we outlined earlier in this chapter and see how they are reflected in Zaccheus's story:

Make Straight the Path: Zaccheus's Version

1. *Did Zaccheus make a searching and fearless moral inventory of his life?* Yes, he was obviously reflecting deeply on every aspect of his life throughout his encounter with Jesus. He didn't put up a façade.

2. *Did Zaccheus admit to God, to himself, and to other human beings the exact nature of his wrongs and his powerlessness over them before he met Jesus?* Yes—he admitted to being a serial crook!

3. *Did Zaccheus believe, or was he at least open to the idea, that Jesus could make him whole?* Yes—first he made the choice of going to see who this Jesus guy was, and later he welcomed him into his home.

4. *Did Zaccheus make a decision to live the New Commandment of loving one's neighbor as Jesus has loved us?* Yes—he sent himself to the poorhouse out of love for his neighbor and trusted that God would take care of all his needs.

5. *Did Zaccheus express a willingness to make amends to anyone he had harmed along the way with his selfish pursuits?* Yes—in spades.

6. *Did Zaccheus make a practical plan to hold himself accountable to God and to others for his future actions?* Yes—he obviously told the apostles about the amazing dinner he had with Jesus and the commitments he made. Otherwise, neither Luke nor we would ever have known his story. We can guess he became a member of the early church community and found there support for his resolutions.

Back to Jim and Samantha, in whom we find a contemporary witness to the power of the same godly self-help as we saw in Zaccheus. During our second or third meeting, I introduced Jim to the Make Straight the Path process, the best place to begin the lifetime journey of being a Junior Partner of the Holy Spirit. This is where we start, no matter how close or far we are from being immersed and walking in God's aid through "baptism in the Spirit"—the lifestyle of flourishing men and women of God who have encountered the Divine Cure, which I also call the Faith-Hope-Love Cure.

The courage to recognize our faults for what they are, to describe them in high-definition clarity, and to admit to ourselves, God, and others that we are powerless over them (the work of the first two steps) doesn't come spontaneously. Many smart people live in denial of their attachment to unhealthy behavior patterns for most if not all of their lives. Have you ever heard a spouse say, "I know he'll [she'll] never change"? Sometimes that's right. Clarity and courage require a willingness to confront our demons, and some people never do it. Many people get through the first two path-preparing steps only after a big personal failure breaks their pride or through the intervention of an honest friend or by an exceptional grace from God.

I bring us back to Jim and Samantha because certainly we can't imitate Zaccheus's great act of humility and trust in Jesus (steps 3 and 4) or his admirable generosity (steps 5 and 6) without the assistance of the Holy Spirit. This is what Jim and Samantha needed—a miracle, a little miracle of Holy Spirit action.

The scare of losing Samantha was the catalyst for Jim's initial awakening to his problem. He would not have contacted me had he not made some sort of moral inventory of his life and recognized some wrongdoing. But as time would tell, Jim's inventory was not yet *searching* and *fearless*. For the next couple of months, Samantha and Jim broke up and got together again almost every other day. Jim was doing back flips, even spiritual back flips, to show Samantha he was a new man. And yet he kept lying about stupid things, as dictated by his seemingly uncontrollable habit. Samantha's own insecurity kept her coming back to Jim even after she'd promised herself and Jim that she would never talk to him again.

At the root of Samantha's insecurity was the thought that she needed all or nothing. She was looking for a perfect Jim, one who would always be true to her and make her happy, or she didn't want him at all. She needed someone else to make her happy, and she was convinced that another imperfect, insecure person like herself could never do that. But then, when alone and feeling lonely, she realized that being without Jim was even more impossible than being with him, for alone she felt even more insecure.

Many couples like Jim and Samantha spend decades fighting. They don't leave each other, because they think someday they will "fix" the other person and all will be well. Only when both partners make straight their own path will they find peace in living with an imperfect person or in moving on to a healthier relationship. We will see later how Jim and Samantha got along.

It's important to note that this divine assistance in path-straightening is not the Faith-Hope-Love Cure itself. It is simply God inviting us and sustaining us as we get our nature ready to be transformed by his grace. In other words, if you have begun to make straight the path and already have new freedom, you can be sure there is much more to come through the Divine Cure.

We have one more step, however, before delving into the Faith-Hope-Love Cure. What happens when we get stuck and simply cannot make straight the path, even when we want to? Throughout my pastoral experience I have witnessed people who, despite great will to move away from their self-destructive patterns, simply *can't*. Something holds them back. It's as if there were another force greater than themselves that prohibited real self-help. Such a force does exist. In the next chapter we will talk about how to free ourselves from the power of Satan, who tries to keep us down with the strength of his lies.

CHAPTER 3

Getting Unstuck

D ivine inner transformation doesn't happen uniformly in every
soul. For some, developing natural mechanisms of self-help such
as honesty, hard work, self-discipline, mind and imagination manage-
ment, and willpower will lead naturally into the domain of God-help,
which in turn will quickly afford the freedom and happiness God is
waiting to give. Others, however, will experience blockage at every turn.
They will feel stuck and powerless even after having formed admirable
human virtue through the steps of path-straightening and after turning
their lives over to the grace of God in the Divine Cure. In these cases,
we ask, "Why do I still react like this?" "Why do I think and talk like
this?" "Why can't I stop being shallow, fearful, shameful, and selfish?"
"Why am I not happy?!"

This blockage feels like powerlessness over negative thought and
behavior patterns. When we are stuck, we *know* what's right and yet
we do the opposite. Even though we want to believe, trust, and love,

we simply can't; or those theological virtues are so weak within us that they can hardly be considered transforming.

THE DEVIL

When we get stuck in our spiritual life and don't know why, a good place to turn is to the devil, also known by the name Satan. The enemy of our soul, he is engaged in our demise.

I haven't made mention yet of the devil because I think one of his methods is to make himself more interesting than he is. If we give too much credit to his influence over us, we will be tempted to take our eyes off Jesus. It is important, nonetheless, to take into account the devil's desire and strategy for our own self-destruction. The devil's existence and action in the world is a fundamental teaching of Christianity, even if you don't hear much about him from the pulpit. If we ignore this teaching, we will never understand the big picture of what is happening around us.

Jesus describes the devil as the father of lies, because the devil says things about us, about others, and about the meaning of life that are not true. "[He] . . . does not stand in the truth," says Jesus, "because there is no truth in him. When he lies, he speaks according to his own nature, for he is a liar and the father of lies" (John 8:44, NRSV). Chances are you don't think much about the devil and his action in your life, and that's probably a healthy choice. But do you believe that he is interested in your soul? Do you believe that he roams the world, "seeking whom he can devour" (1 Pet. 5:8, KJV)?

Curiously, I have found in nonreligious circles an acute belief in and awareness of supernatural evil, "the dark side," and even the devil. A few years ago I was asked to do some minor consulting for a Hollywood production that included a scene of exorcism—the traditional ritual of the Catholic Church in which a properly appointed minister asks God to release someone from demonic possession. After being convinced that the director and producers were interested in portraying the scene in an honest and respectful way, I agreed to offer my advice. (I didn't allow them to use my name, however, because I didn't want to affiliate myself with a project whose content I couldn't control.) We met in a dimly lit lounge area on the top floor of an old hotel in Rome. A corner of the room was set aside for my meeting with the director, the executive producer, and the main actor. We sat on couches around a low marble table. The lounge was sprinkled with other guests, but I assumed we were the only ones in the room involved in the production.

In the initial formalities and salutations, I hoped to get a feel for who I was working with. The lead actor gave me a perfect opportunity when he asked, "So what do we call you—'Jonathan,' 'Father,' . . . ?"

"If you like, you can call me Father Jonathan," I responded. I then used that exchange as an opening to ask them about *their* religious backgrounds. I learned that one was "culturally Jewish" and the others were "nothing in particular."

As soon as we sat down, the director got straight to the point, "Do you believe in the devil, Father Jonathan?"

"Yes, I do," I responded.

"Do you think he can possess someone?"

"Yep, I've seen it, but it's very rare."

"Why so rare?"

"Well, he's usually a bit smarter. He gets involved in our lives under the radar and works ceaselessly to lead us astray, away from God."

Out of the corner of my eye, I noticed there were now two or three additional people standing not far from our table, almost directly behind me. I signaled their presence to the executive producer with a nod. He lifted his hand just off the table as if to say it was all okay.

"And what about you all—do you believe in the devil?" I asked.

To my surprise, this group of practical atheists, all three of them, responded in the affirmative. The irony hit me: they didn't believe in God, but they believed in the devil!

For the next fifteen minutes we talked about the presence of evil in the world. As we did, more and more of those in the room gathered around us to listen in as we sat in our little corner. It turned out that *everyone* in the room was affiliated with the project, and they *all* wanted to hear and talk about the devil! They knew him because they had felt his presence, they had seen his works.

The greatest tool of the devil is deceit. We have seen how the pedagogy of God is to involve us in his master plan for redemption. The devil's pedagogy is to make us active participants in our own damnation.

If we ignore the devil's ability to influence our minds and wreak serious havoc on them, we will always be missing an important factor in the equation of emotional and spiritual healing. He is actively working to sow doubt and confusion. The devil's lies do damage!

REACTIONS THAT POINT TO THE DEVIL'S WORK

In *The Promise* I used two examples that I think are worth telling again here, for they exemplify both the singular power of the devil's lies to hold us down and the still more powerful grace of God to free us from their bondage and heal us of the wounds they inflict. The first story is about a seminarian, Sam, whom I taught in Rome and who was struggling with deep feelings of insecurity, for no apparent reason.

The second was about a family friend, whom I called Mary, who had suffered sexual abuse as a young woman and who was near the point of a mental breakdown as a result.

Let's look at Sam first. There was no apparent reason for his indecisiveness and insecurity. Not only was he a great guy, Sam was smarter, better prepared, more athletic and good-looking, and more spiritual than many of his seminary classmates. In his early twenties he had encountered Jesus in a profound way, and he went through a deep process of conversion that included, in effect, the six Make Straight the Path steps described earlier. In other words, he was right with God and with others. He was on a path of total service to God and the Catholic Church. And *still* he was insecure.

Sam initially told me he had "always been like this," but after several conversations over a period of a few months, I asked Sam to reconsider this. As far as I could see, he had no real reason to be fearful or shameful. His considerable talent and goodness were evident to everyone but himself. Sam agreed to reflect and, above all, to ask God to show him the origin of his long-held feelings of inadequacy.

Sensing a need for God's grace to heal old wounds, I suggested that Sam ask Christ to remind him of times in his past when these feelings of inadequacy had been particularly intense. He laughed. "I think I can tell you now, even though I don't like talking about it," he said. Sam recounted how he was very popular in junior high school and a solid member of the in-crowd. About halfway through the year, he became the first guy to have a girlfriend, and she was the prettiest girl in the class. One day soon after, he went to school and none of his friends would talk to him. They had simply stopped being his friends, just like that. They were apparently jealous of his luck with the girls, and as revenge, from one day to the next they tuned him out.

"I couldn't believe it," he told me, obviously moved by the memory. "These guys were supposedly my friends!"

Sam's life changed on that day. He shut down on the inside, while maintaining an outward presence of being cool and indifferent. He no longer trusted classmates, girls, or even, to some extent, lifelong friends. The possibility of a similar moment of rejection was enough to make sure he never made himself vulnerable to others in the same way again.

False Perceptions as the Genesis of Lies

Kids can be pretty cruel, but they don't betray people in the same malicious way adults do. If we could watch a replay of what happened to Sam—what his friends actually did and how they executed it—we would surely stand in wonderment at Sam's disproportionately negative reaction. No matter how mean these kids' words and actions may have been, they couldn't possibly merit the life-altering attitude Sam adopted in the wake of the event.

So what happened? I don't know for sure, nor does Sam. But on account of some personal weakness (emotional immaturity, lack of relationship experience, previous trauma?), he perceived the event in a false way, a way that didn't correspond to reality. That can happen to any of us, but it happens especially to children. Misinterpretation of an event's meaning doesn't suggest that evil is at work. What *is* a common sign of the devil's handiwork, however, is that Sam lived the misinterpreted event as definitive and dramatic. In his mind, his relationship with these "idyllic" friends went from perfect to zero overnight, and if they were such good friends and yet could betray him, *nobody* could be trusted going forward.

Now, as an adult, Sam saw just as clearly as I did how his original perception of the event was probably warped—and even if it wasn't, its effect on his future was certainly disproportionate. I referred him to Bible passages and good spiritual reading as an aid to renew his mind.

Accepting his internal exaggeration of the event was helpful to Sam, but nevertheless it didn't get rid of the problem. This is the devil's power: his lies stick; they seep into the marrow of our spiritual bones, warping our vision of reality. The result is emotional and spiritual damage. And when there *is* damage, a third person setting the record straight (even when backed by the Bible) can help, but as we'll see it's not usually enough.

Buying into Lies

I encouraged Sam not to think too much about all of this. Drumming up in our own minds negative experiences from the past is usually not very productive. What I did suggest was that in his usual time of daily prayer, he dialogue with Jesus and ask him for light and help about every aspect of his life, including this negative experience.

A week later when Sam came back to talk he was very different. He was smiling! He stood three feet in front of me—not the usual ten (a "safe" distance)—and he spoke with confidence and peace. It was clear he was no longer guarding every word, measuring every response. He put it like this: "In prayer, when I asked God what he thought about all those negative feelings, it came to me so clearly. Those guys didn't really hate me. They were just being kids. And the uselessness, inadequacy, and all of that—that's not true either. God made me and he loves me and that's enough."

Sam recounted this as if it were earth-shattering. But to me it sounded so simple, and if I didn't know better, I would say even simplistic. He and I had talked through these very truths he was telling me. He had read all the Bible passages about God's love for him. What had happened *this* time to make a difference? Why, from one day to the next, did Sam experience an inner peace and freedom he had not felt in many years? God was able to enter Sam's life in an integral way. He was able to speak truth to Sam not with ideas or concepts, but with his healing grace. Because the truths came from God, in the form of grace, Sam experienced real mind and heart renewal.

Let's review Sam's simple journey:

Step 1. He recognized that his feelings were incongruent with reality (irrational) and were somehow related to a past event or series of events.

Step 2. He accepted that the related events from the past were only the occasion, not the actual cause, of the real damage; the damage was caused by his belief in the lies about himself.

Step 3. He aided the renewal of his mind and heart by asking for help from someone he trusted and looking to the Word of God.

Step 4. In prayer, God showed him the specific lies he had accepted and instantly (even if only partially) freed him from their bondage.

THE VULNERABILITY OF TRAUMA AND PAIN

In moments of particular weakness, pain, or trauma, we are more susceptible to believing mistruths. Our increased sensibility in these moments is fertile ground for the devil to embed his lies deeply into our souls, as our second example from *The Promise* illustrates.

Mary came from an upper-middle-class Christian family. She had several brothers and sisters, and parents who had been married happily for over forty years. But Mary was always getting sick. Throughout her teenage and young adult years she suffered various physical and emotional illnesses that baffled every doctor who treated her. They found no link. Some said it was all in her head.

A few years later, with the help of a good psychologist, Mary began to recall systematic sexual abuse during her childhood by a neighbor. Several independent psychologists concurred that the memories were probably real. Real or not, Mary became increasingly concerned and unstable. She wasn't the kind of person to make anything up, to accuse anyone falsely, or to grieve about something that might never have occurred. She was pretty sure, however, that whatever had happened was the origin of her other problems. Unless she worked this out, there would be no closure and she would never be healthy.

The "pain," as she referred to it, came at the most unexpected times: riding the London Underground, talking on the phone with a friend, even sitting quietly in church. Often the pain felt like failure. But it wasn't a failure of the past—the kind that says, "You messed up." It was an existential and permanent failure—"You don't matter." Other times the pain felt like sin—"It's your fault," "You shouldn't be so nice," "You lead people on," "You're dirty," "You're stupid."

Whatever the feeling of the day, it was always self-accusatory. At the height of her struggle, the past, present, and future were all pretty much the same to Mary: "Because of what happened—or didn't happen—or will happen—I'm always going to be like this, and because I am, I'm always going to make other people suffer."

Replacing Lies with Truth

Mary's road to healing is a happy one, thank God. It wasn't fast, but it was solid and it has lasted. In Mary's road to healing you will be able to identify the same four steps I just described in talking about Sam's journey. She lived them in a slightly different order, in a less linear fashion, and because of the depth of the damage, she moved through them more slowly.

As in Sam's case, Mary's Christian formation was very solid. Unlike Sam, she never had a major conversion. Because she never had any major self-destructive behavior patterns to confront, her attempts to make straight the path were unconscious and continuous. She was right with God and with everyone currently in her life. She believed, hoped, and loved with great sincerity. But Mary brewed in sadness, anger, and despair on account of a ghost from the past. Unwittingly, she had traded in the gifts of freedom and self-determination for the right to live in perpetual misery . . . because *someone else* had entered and taken control of her life.

Mary came to me out of desperation. Psychologists and therapists had helped her in a respectful and nonmanipulative way to recall the sexual abuse. She was relieved to have pinpointed a starting point of her interior confusion and pain (damage).

This was step 1—she had identified the related event. But the pain had not gone away. Was she going to have to live like this forever? As we talked through her story, it became clear that she had already made significant progress. She recounted how at first she had looked for inner peace in the offending neighbor's eventual repentance or acknowledgment of wrongdoing. With the good advice and help of professionals, she put that false hope aside as unhealthy and unrealistic, not only because it might never happen, but most importantly because even if it were to happen, it wouldn't completely heal the wounds.

Talking to Mary, I could see she had a truly beautiful soul. Her suffering was particularly deep because she had once experienced the beauty of emotional and spiritual wholeness. She longed to recover the innocence of her early childhood and the harmony of her family life.

"What's the hardest thing in dealing with all of this?" I asked her.

"It's the pain that comes out of the blue," she replied.

"What do you mean by 'pain'? Is it physical?"

She didn't need to think long to give an answer. She had obviously done plenty of that already. "Yes and no. I feel it coming on, sometimes like a hot dagger, sometimes like a slow fever, and usually like a quick, cold jolt. But I know the pain isn't caused by anything physical because it comes out of the blue, and in all different circumstances."

I could tell Mary was besieged by lies about herself.

"After the pain leaves, how do you feel?"

"I feel like I always do, but just more intensely, I guess—worse."

"And how does that feel?" I continued.

Mary lowered her glance. "I feel like I'm dirty, useless, and alone."

"And *are* you all those things?" I asked.

"That's how I *feel*," she said, and then she cried.

Because I knew Mary's family and I was beginning to get to know her as well, I knew that none of what she felt was true. She wasn't dirty, she wasn't useless, and she wasn't alone.

For the next several months we worked on identifying the lies for what they were. We weren't looking to get rid of them just yet. Mary knew on an intellectual level that she had done nothing wrong to become "dirty"; she had many gifts and talents to offer the world, and she was surrounded by family and friends who loved her dearly. But when she felt the pain . . . there was the lie.

It was hard—almost impossible at first—for Mary to see that the pain did not cause the dreadful thoughts, but rather that the thoughts (fear induced by lies about herself) caused the pain. Psychological stimulants, often uncontrollable, were provoking subconscious fears— fear of dirtiness, uselessness, and loneliness, among others. Mary didn't experience any of this as fear. For her it was just pain, a quasi-physical pain of some sort. She described the yucky feelings which followed the pain as shameful statements of truth about herself. Only later did she come to understand these "postpain" feelings as residue from the same work of the lie-induced fear.

One simple practice which helped Mary, and has helped many others, was to examine the dynamics of her mind and heart as soon as possible after the actual experience of fear and pain. I suggested she keep a disposable journal. When she felt the pain coming on, she learned to be attentive to the accompanying lie. She wrote down each phrase in a little blue notebook. I suggested she title it "The Little Book of Big Lies."

Over time we talked through each flagrant lie in that little book. I asked her where the thoughts came from, whether she believed them, and if she wanted them to control her mind.

Mary didn't know where they came from, she didn't really believe them (at least not intellectually), and no, she didn't want them to have free rein in her life.

Next to each lie in her book, together we wrote down the real deal about who she is and why she is of inestimable worth, a worth which can never be destroyed. For the next few months, Mary substituted the spontaneous bad thoughts with the truths we both believed.

We decided to use Bible passages to call to mind fundamental truths about herself, God, and others. This was step 3—she asked for help from someone she trusted and looked to the Word of God for light.

- *I have no friends.* "I no longer call you slaves, because a slave does not know what his master is doing. I have called you friends, because I have told you everything I have heard from my Father." (John 15:15, NAB)

- *Nobody really knows me for who I am.* "Before I formed you in the womb I knew you, before you were born I dedicated you, a prophet to the nations I appointed you." (Jer. 1:5, NAB)

- *Nobody loves me.* "For I am the Lord, your God, the Holy One of Israel, your savior. I give Egypt as your ransom, Ethiopia and Seba in return for you. Because you are precious in my eyes and glorious, and because I love you, I give men in return for you and peoples in exchange for your life." (Isa. 43:3–4, NAB)

- *It's all my fault.* "For freedom Christ set us free; so stand firm and do not submit again to the yoke of slavery." (Gal. 5:1, NAB)

- *I'm dirty from the inside out.* "What God has made clean, you must not profane." (Acts 10:14, NAB)

- *Things will never get better.* "I, the Lord, have called you for the victory of justice, I have grasped you by the hand; I formed you, and set you as a covenant of the people, a light for the nations." (Isa. 42:6, NAB)

Weeks passed after we did this work together, and I didn't hear from Mary. When she finally called, I could hear in her voice that something had changed. In particular, she told me she now realized that somewhere along the line she had come to believe that her present and future happiness depended entirely on "fixing" what this man had done to her. "That's not true!" she said. "He didn't change me at all. If I live in the truth of who I am and why God loves me, I can take back the reins of my life."

This was step 2—she recognized that the related event was only the occasion, not the actual cause, of the long-term damage. The real damage was caused by the lies she came to believe about herself.

Mary now had new serenity. She told me that she had memorized each of the six passages we had selected in my office, and instead of waiting for the pain to come so that she could replace the accompanying lie-induced thoughts with the biblical truth, she started repeating the verses in her head whenever she had a free moment. That exercise began as mere repetition, she said, but it became prayer. Over and over again she talked to God—not in her old, convoluted thought pattern, but rather in truth.

I was happy for Mary and I told her so. But before we hung up, I warned her that I didn't think this would be the end of her pain. While I believe in the power of God to work miracles in any way he wants, God's grace and power work ordinarily through natural mechanisms. After all, he created these psychological, spiritual, and physical mechanisms for a purpose, and that too is a miracle.

Simply replacing lies with truths (even biblical truths) can help someone establish a semblance of stability in his or her life, and it's a necessary step toward full mind renewal, but when there's deep-seated damage, *knowing* the truth is rarely enough to achieve the full renewal of the mind and healing of the heart. God needs to step in and work a miracle of grace.

Mary agreed that things probably weren't all in order. She still couldn't imagine having an intimate relationship with a man, for example. By passing through the first three steps, though, she was better prepared for God to heal her heart, through prayer, of the lies that hurt her; and eventually she made it through the fourth as well, working with God. Sam's road was relatively quick. Mary, on the other hand, was not yet able, at this stage in her story, to hear clearly the voice of God, because the devil's lies were so deeply embedded in her psyche. She was just beginning to regain a semblance of control over her emotional world. Having learned to replace the mistruths that caused her so much pain with God's Word, she reported an acceptable degree of stability.

This is the status of millions and millions of our contemporaries. Through one technique or another, we learn to get by. We become professionals at dealing with the background music of serious emotional damage. Faith helps some people get by. Others depend on distractions.

I told Mary that I thought there was still a part of her heart and mind that God's healing grace had been unable to transform. *Unable?* Yes, so to speak. God usually holds back his power out of respect for our free will and our natural (God-given) mechanisms. Without us even asking, at any moment he could wipe us clean of any trace of emotional damage. But he doesn't usually do this. He wants us to be intimately involved in our own healing. As scripture tells us, "Ask, and it will be given you; seek, and you will find; knock, and [the door] will be opened to you" (Matt. 7:7, RSV). Mary had asked, searched, and knocked many times. Where were the answers? Why did the door remain shut?

I don't think the door *was* shut. Mary just wasn't well enough to walk through it. Part of God's incredible patience with us can be seen in his respect for our natural healing mechanisms. It is easy to see this with physical healing. Doctors use the gift of intelligence to study medicine. They in turn then teach us how the body works and how to get better. It would be presumptuous to ask a doctor to make us well even as we eat junk food, avoid all exercise, and disregard her medical prescriptions.

It is not altogether different with emotional healing. God respects our psychological mechanisms. When those mechanisms have been violated by poor development or trauma, psychologists and psychiatrists can help us get better through natural means. But as we have already seen, we must also keep in mind that our psychological and emotional world is the devil's playground: "Your enemy the devil prowls around like a roaring lion looking for someone to devour" (1 Pet. 5:8, NIV). Purely natural techniques don't heal supernatural wounds. We need the grace of God.

Medical professionals can point out where and how our psyche has been injured and can offer many helpful techniques for natural healing. But if we leave out of the equation negative, supernatural forces (the devil and his lies) which bind our psyche and keep us down, we will always be slow to turn to positive, supernatural forces (God and his love) to free us from our bondage.

Accepting the Healing Grace of God

Cases like Mary's, where the psychology has been severely damaged through the trauma of sexual abuse, are some of the devil's favorite targets. The aggression against the victims is objectively so terrible that he can lob lies in their direction and those lies almost always stick.

We tend to forget that the "glue" that binds these devilish lies to the victim's mind is not natural. Because it flows from the devil, it is a supernatural substance. It only makes sense (and this has also been my experience) that the most effective dissolvent will be supernatural as well (the healing grace of God).

When I explained these principles to Mary, a lightbulb went on inside her. Her experience with many good psychologists had taught her to be a survivor. But her struggle didn't go away. She was still stuck in the past, and she could now see the nature of the "glue."

I asked her if she wanted to be truly free. I asked her if she was willing to let go of the past and experience freedom-living in the present. These questions are essential because we can get used to being a victim, and if we don't *want* freedom, God won't force it on us. We can become accustomed and even attached to our suffering. We wonder who we would be if we didn't have to deal with this or that issue. God will never free us if we choose to stay stuck.

Mary told me, with a conviction that was palpable, that she wanted God to renew her completely.

Keeping in mind the supernatural realities, I told Mary my hunch was it would be helpful if she were to invite God in prayer to show her precisely what was holding her down, and to do this in a certain way. Through the help of good psychologists, Mary was ahead of the game here: she didn't need to pinpoint the related event; she already had identified the traumatic event of sexual abuse as the starting point of her suffering. What she still may not have known, I suggested, was why that distant event had power over her in the present. As I had done with Sam, I suggested she take more time for prayer and invite God to help her relive those hurtful moments from the past in his presence and truth. I encouraged her not to be afraid to actually feel again what she felt back then, if that's what God wanted.

Mary reported to me that the first time she prayed like this, she experienced peace like she had never known before. She didn't get any miraculous visions or even learn any new truths about her situation. But it was through reliving in the presence of Jesus on an intellectual and emotional level the terrible moments of her past that a new spiritual freedom was released in her—finally, step 4. She had asked God for help many times before, but she had never opened her heart to him in such a complete way.

In prayer she experienced with the certainty of faith that "God was with me even in the moment of abuse, and he is with me now. I am not alone." Over several months, every time something triggered the pain, she looked for a quiet place to pray—even for just one or two minutes. She would turn those feelings from the past or the present over to God and ask him what he had to say about them. Sometimes she heard God speak to her—"I love you," "Trust in me," and so on—but most of the time she just stayed in his quiet presence. Each and every time she turned to him with her whole being, God was healing her heart.

Many months later, Mary is still in awe of how the things which used to trigger the pain now come and go with almost no effect. Like Sam, Mary allowed God to work in her spiritual, intellectual, and emotional life in a natural and holistic way. With no suggestive or manipulative interference from anyone, God used the mechanisms he created of memory and emotion to bring to Sam's and Mary's minds events from the past that were related to present emotional and spiritual suffering—and he will do the same for us. When we open those areas we have kept hidden, God will enter and heal.

What I'm describing here is not so much a new method of prayer and recovery as it is a simple deduction from what we already know through human experience and Christian doctrine. I'm inviting you to tap in to the way God made us. By following these principles, we are preparing our natural mechanisms of the mind and emotions to be open to the very "ordinary" miracle of complete mind-renewal.

PRAYER METHODOLOGY: TRACKING THE SOURCE OF DAMAGING LIES

The writings of Christian psychologist and counselor Dr. Edward Smith (a Southern Baptist who wrote *Healing Life's Hurts Through Theophostic Prayer*) and Fr. David Tickerhoof (a Catholic priest who wrote *A Catholic's Guide to Theophostic Prayer Ministry*) have confirmed and shed light on the spiritual principles I have described above.

Dr. Smith developed a "prayer methodology" known as "theophostic prayer"—that first word meaning "God's light"—which involves a trained counselor accompanying another person as he or she seeks help from God to source the lies that have caused inner damage. Dr. Smith insists that this method should never involve suggestive or manipulative coaching. The leader simply invites the person to ask God for help to "follow the smoke" from the present negative emotion (anger, fear, resentment) to emotions of a similar feel from the past.

If we allow ourselves, explains Dr. Smith—and especially if we ask God for his help in prayer—we will remember moments in the past that felt similar to the negative emotions we are dealing with in the present. Related events have "matching feelings," even if they are years apart. If a woman, for example, is gripped with fear every time her husband gets up and walks away silently from a heated conversation, in prayer she can ask God to show her moments from her past where she had similar feelings of fearful abandonment. She will usually find that her husband is not causing the extreme fear; his actions are triggering lingering fears from the past. By "following the smoke" in prayer, she can pinpoint this unresolved damage.

Dr. Smith insists this is not an exercise of therapeutic memory recall. It is allowing the God-given mechanisms of the mind to point to related events. What's new in Dr. Smith's approach is the method of pinpointing the connection: he uses the natural mechanism of "following the smoke" to cooperate with God in his desire to indicate to us what event from the past is related to the current difficulty.

A second step of Dr. Smith's methodology involves confronting the unresolved damage. Once a person has pinpointed the related event, the trained counselor encourages the person to relive that moment and its corresponding emotions and to talk about what he or she is feeling. Then the counselor invites the person to ask God what *he* thinks of that past event (again, without making any suggestions or insinuations about what God's mind on the matter might be).

Many people who have followed this prayer methodology with the aid of a trained professional have experienced marvelous healing as God reveals his truth and renews their minds and hearts.

Whether you find this particular prayer method helpful will depend greatly on your background and spiritual sensibilities. It seems of particular relevance in cases where inner damage is so severe that a person is unable on his or her own to penetrate emotional barriers.

Regardless, I think that the two primary underlying principles of this method are solid and can be helpful to all of us in our personal prayer:

1. With the help of God we can easily discover the connection between disproportionate negative emotions surrounding a present difficulty and the related events from the past by

"following the smoke" (recalling in prayer emotions of the same "feel").

2. When we allow God to speak to us about these past events, on a spiritual, intellectual, and emotional level, his word of truth comes with healing power.

DISCERNMENT: RECOGNIZING GOD'S VOICE

If proper interpretation of scripture is essential in order to understand the full meaning of God's Word (as we discussed earlier), even more important is proper discernment in our own prayer, because here there is more room for subjective error. What if Sam and Mary had "heard in prayer" that, for example, God didn't really love them? What if they had come back with an even deeper conviction of their *uselessness*, this time "seconded" by God himself?

Because we are spiritually hard of hearing, we can easily make such mistakes. Sometimes we think we hear God's voice, and we simply get it wrong.

How do we recognize and discern God's voice? I recommend three things to start with:

1. Read and contemplate sacred scripture.

2. Study sound Christian doctrine.

3. Ask for guidance from a prudent and holy person who will speak the truth to you even when it hurts.

As in most things, there is a danger here of placing too much importance on our feelings, on past events, and on spiritual and emotional damage. We can start thinking and acting as if everything we feel, believe, and do is dependent on or even determined by the past. This is simply not true.

It is important to find a balance between seeking healing of the wounds which are holding us back, on the one hand, and leaving the past behind us and moving forward in faith, on the other.

Now, as we begin the second part of this book, we will go deeper into what the theological virtues of faith, hope, and love look like in our lives when they become new dispositions of the heart. We can call these new dispositions *living faith, living hope,* and *living love.* They are direct and perfect responses to our negative mega-patterns of shallowness, fear and shame, and self-centeredness. It is no coincidence that these dispositions sound active. As Junior Partners of the Holy Spirit, we have the option of taking advantage of God's gifts of faith, hope, and love. It is in *living* the theological virtues that we become spirit-filled.

Before addressing these virtues, each in its own chapter, I first want to peel away the blinders that most of us have set up along our personal journey. These blinders are barricades that keep us going in the same direction, at the same speed, without imagining our potential for game-changing redirection and growth through *living faith, living hope,* and *living love.*

We are now entering the heart of the Divine Cure.

PART 2

The Faith-Hope-Love Cure

CHAPTER 4

Introduction to the Divine Cure

Although she looked familiar, I wasn't sure I knew her. The congregation was moving quickly out the church doors into the courtyard after my Sunday evening service. I was brand new to the parish and focused on greeting the regulars and introducing myself to the newcomers. Sarah—as I later learned her name to be—stood quietly off to the side, nervously shifting her weight from one leg to the other and occasionally reaching up with one hand to rearrange her long brown hair over the front of her shoulder, only to push it back again a moment later.

From Sarah's body language I knew she was looking for a way to tell me she needed to talk. As she approached, she blurted out, "I'm not really sure why I wanted to talk to you, but since moving here to New York City, I haven't been going to church every week, and I *have* to get back into it. So I came tonight, and I'll come back every week, I promise!"

"You're very welcome here," I responded, "but you don't have to promise me anything. Just do your best." I surprised myself with my response, which felt wishy-washy. *Where did that come from?* I wondered.

Instantly the young woman's demeanor changed, and dramatically. "I don't have to promise?" she asked with a smile as she tilted her head back and let out the loudest sigh of relief I've ever heard. "Phew!"

"No, just do your best," I repeated. I knew she could misunderstand me to be saying church attendance didn't matter, but I said it again because I knew that her transformation from ultratense to beautifully peaceful, almost euphoric, could only be the fruit of God working in her soul.

Sarah did come back the following week, and now not only do I see her at the weekly service, but she is involved in all sorts of parish projects and activities. She is spontaneous and joyful, and she always laughs when I joke with her that she is forbidden to make any promises about coming the next week. She knows it's both a joke and not a joke—she needs to hear it.

Months after our first encounter, Sarah introduced me to her parents, Mr. and Mrs. McGrath, who were visiting from the Midwest. It was then I finally understood the inner dynamics of Sarah's story. Her parents approached me nervously, and before I could even greet them they blurted out a litany of the church activities and charitable projects they were involved with back home; then they launched into how they'd raised all of their kids to be good Christians, etc. The other people standing around seemed a bit uncomfortable with the overly religious introduction, but it didn't bother me at all, for sometimes people are just a bit nervous when they meet a new pastor or priest and don't know what else to say.

Over the next week I had the pleasure of sharing a string of meals with Sarah and her family—something I rarely have or take the time to do—and the result was most enriching! The family fireworks began with an innocent question from Sarah's mom, who, after an otherwise pleasant conversation, asked me in the most serious of tones—in front of Sarah and her dad—when precisely Sarah had begun to attend my church and if she'd attended every Sunday since. I tried to sidestep the question with some humor, but I quickly realized that lightheartedness wasn't going to work. Her dad chimed in with the same question, in more direct fashion: "When did Sarah first come to your church?"

I looked over at Sarah with the hope of finding a reassuring smile which would convey that this was all an inside family joke. Aware of my predicament, and with her newfound spiritual confidence, she jumped in with great candor, laying the cards on the table: "Mom and Dad, before moving to New York I had already decided I wasn't going to go to church; so when I got here, I didn't go. It wasn't until a few months ago—after almost two years in the city—that I went to my first mass at St. Patrick's Old Cathedral. It was just a fluke. I hadn't planned on coming back. And by the way, I don't think Mark and Allie are going to church either."

My heart dropped. Mr. and Mrs. McGrath's pride and joy was obviously the "Christian practice" of their children. From Sarah's tone and expression, I assumed (correctly) that Mark and Allie were her brother and sister.

"That's not true," chimed in her mother. "Both Mark and Allie have been attending Sunday services since they left home."

"Okay," responded Sarah. "I'm now probably in trouble both with them and with you, but Mom and Dad, I must break it to you, they're just as disillusioned with God and church as I have been for the last few years, and they're still just as scared to tell you about it as I am relieved to be telling you this now!"

I felt like excusing myself to use the restroom, but that would have been too conspicuous. Instead, I tried to fade into the background, bowing my head slightly and folding my hands.

That was the beginning of three days of deep discussion between Sarah and her parents. In the evenings, I would connect with them and hear a summary of what had gone down during the day. I don't think I've ever spent that much time, in such a short period of time, with a single family—especially one that I didn't know very well previously. But I found myself in the middle of it, and I felt that this was probably where God would have me. Lots of tears were exchanged that week, but Sarah took to heart the advice to avoid sharp, cutting, and hurtful words that break down communication and leave scars. She was able to do this only because of the spiritual freedom she had discovered over the previous few months. The core of the family issue was deep resentment for what Sarah and her siblings perceived as a force-fed, rigid religiosity that was less about faith, hope, and love and more about rules. This resulted in fear, guilt, and shame.

This is not to say Mr. and Mrs. McGrath weren't good people— they were incredibly good people! They were living their faith in a similar way to the rich young man in Mark's Gospel. Like that man, whom we considered in this book's introduction, they could have responded honestly to Jesus, "Teacher, we have kept all these [commandments] since our youth." And like that rich young man, who knew deep down that he was still missing something, this couple knew this too. Their admirable moral living had not yet become for them a source of joy and fulfillment, and their kids knew it. Maybe Jesus would have looked at them, loved them, and said, "You lack one thing;

go, stop worrying about being so darn perfect; then come follow me."

The ideal that Jesus holds out to us is very, very high, but we miss the point of human flourishing—living as spirit-filled men and woman—if we confuse his plan for us with mere human perfection. Jesus is interested in our becoming more like him, more like his Father, and that kind of transformation can happen only in the heart and only through the infusion of God's grace. Genuine Christian perfection, then, is all *gift*. We can, and must, prepare ourselves to receive the gift through living righteously—especially living the cardinal virtues of prudence, fortitude, temperance, and justice—but these virtues, or any other set of virtues, even if we practice them "perfectly," will not make us perfect!

Jesus made clear the distinction between false human perfection and real perfection when he said to his disciples, "Be perfect, therefore, as your heavenly Father is perfect." Let's read those words in context:

> But I say to you, Love your enemies and pray for those who persecute you, so that you may be children of your Father in heaven; for he makes his sun rise on the evil and on the good, and sends rain on the righteous and on the unrighteous. For if you love those who love you, what reward do you have? Do not even the tax collectors do the same? And if you greet only your brothers and sisters, what more are you doing than others? Do not even the Gentiles do the same? Be perfect, therefore, *as your heavenly Father is perfect*. (Matt. 44–48, NRSV, emphasis added)

Jesus is telling the disciples, and us today, that loving others—everyone—in the way his Father loves us, unconditionally and for the sake of the other (not for what we can get from the person or for the good feelings that come when we do the right thing) is the *sign* of Christian perfection.

Is that possible? Is it possible to love that much, to love like God?

You already know the answer from our discussion of the rich young man: "For mortals it is impossible, but not for God; with God all things are possible" (Mark 10:27, NRSV).

But we also know that this doesn't mean we're off the hook. It doesn't mean that our becoming spirit-filled will be a random act of God. God is depending on us, as Junior Partners of the Spirit, to do some of the prep work to get our hearts ready for him to work the miracle of helping us love everyone as he loves us.

This miracle is a healing of our heart. It is a reordering by God's grace of our disordered passions; it is an aligning of our soul with our final destiny of living as saints in heaven. This is precisely what happened to Sarah: the barriers to God's grace that she had built up to defend herself from what she considered the untenable demands of religion were broken down by her encounter with a community that was living real faith, hope, and love. She still was holding on to anger and resentment against her parents that would require significant healing, but at least the walls against God's grace had already been toppled. For most people, these barriers come down more slowly, the miracle happening in stages, but Sarah's transformation was a testimony to God's power and will to act quickly, if we let him.

In another chapter we will pick up the story of the McGrath family again. God's grace eventually brought healing and great happiness to all of them. Their journey is worth knowing and has clues for how God wants to heal us.

Our collaboration with the miracle of true happiness does not have to be complicated. It is indeed remarkably simple. It is the honest and intentional acceptance and living of faith, hope, and love in the nitty-gritty of our daily lives. Theologians call these the "theological virtues" because they relate us directly to God; "human virtues," on the other hand—such as honesty, hard work, and courage—can do no more than make us good people. The theological virtues, when we let them, transform us from within into the wonderful, beautiful, holy sons and daughters of God we were created to be. When we accept these gifts from God, they get us ready to live in a personal relationship with the Holy Trinity—Father, Son, and Holy Spirit. Anyone with that kind of relationship will be spirit-filled.

THE NEED FOR A PARADIGM SHIFT

Do you find it hard (or even impossible) to be spirit-filled when things are going terribly wrong and everything we see on television, read in books, and even hear from good friends points us toward skepticism, bitterness, and self-absorption?

Having lived many years in Europe and studied some of its art, music, and history, I'm reminded that people haven't always lived in an aggressively anti-Christian culture like ours, which attempts to drain us of the Spirit of God. Perhaps it's a bit much to say the Middle Ages were a "Golden Age" for Christianity, for that period had its own set of inglorious moments, but we can certainly identify a time and region in history—"Christendom"—when and where society (politicians, legislators, artists, educators, etc.) promoted the Christian lifestyle as an ideal, even if its members and projects were far from perfect. Perhaps if we had been born in those times, there would have been no need for this book. We would have been reminded of truth, goodness, and beauty at most turns, imbibing them through the culture, and thus we would have been freer to make courageous choices in line with the theological virtues to which they direct us—faith, hope, and love.

Yes, times have changed. Our ideas of truth, goodness, and beauty are garbled, and for the most part we have no idea what theological virtues are. Imagine the spectrum of answers you would get if you were to ask your colleagues for a definition of faith, hope, or love! We need to be reeducated in all things spiritual. Since the 1960s, pop culture, secular academia, and much of the media have waged an effective campaign against traditional morality and belief. I see no conspiracy here: it's just the logical result of several spiritually confused generations spreading their wings. Rather than jumping on the bandwagon of blaming the cult of sex, drugs, and rock and roll for our present condition, let's take a step back and remember the 30s, 40s, and 50s. Really, how strong was America's Christian culture then, and what was holding it together? When one generation teaches another generation by word or example that "being Christian" has more to do with rules and regulations, appearances and image, than with vibrant and practical faith, hope, and love, that next generation will have every reason to rebel. The rebellion of the 60s was not a movement away from real faith and religion, but rather a shift away from stifling impostors of faith and religion that were perpetuated in preceding decades.

If we are to create a healthier, God-centered home, neighborhood, and country for our children and grandchildren, we need to give them reasons for believing. If we are to pass on true spirituality, we need to understand it and live it as the source of all we do. We need a paradigm shift toward living out the theological virtues of faith, hope, and love on a daily basis.

With this reeducation in spirituality in mind, I will offer a simple model for spiritual growth and personal fulfillment. I've employed new language designed to connect with our contemporary experience, but the spiritual paradigm itself is one and the same with Jesus's fundamental teachings. The new language is incorporated into a unique approach that will help us break free from long-cultivated, self-destructive patterns and tap into our huge spiritual potential.

The approach is quite simple. My work over the years as a spiritual counselor has allowed me to identify three mega-patterns of self-destructive thought and behavior. All of our specific struggles can be traced back to one of these.

1. Shallowness

2. Fear, anxiety, and shame

3. Self-centeredness

Breaking free from the grip of these three mega-patterns involves transferring our spiritual energy away from fixing our failures and toward our divine calling and destiny: resting in the heart of God through participation in his divine life. This approach will invite you to forge three new "dispositions of the heart," lifestyle remedies for the three mega-patterns named above.

The three new dispositions of the heart—living faith, living hope, and living love—can redeem our warped inclinations by healing our reason, memory, and will.

The spiritual journey of this book can be summarized in this way:

1. From shallowness to living faith by a healing of our intellect

2. From fear, anxiety, and shame to living hope by a healing of our memory

3. From self-centeredness to living love by a healing of our will

From here on out I will point to the Faith-Hope-Love Cure—the Divine Cure—at every turn. Learning to claim this cure in each of its three parts is the essence of our journey toward becoming spirit-filled people. The cure is valid for each and every one of us, no matter what self-destructive or self-limiting patterns we are struggling with. While the specific approach we take in this book for learning the Faith-Hope-Love Cure is mine, and just one among many valid approaches, the cure itself is *the* way God saves us and brings us to personal fulfillment.

I think the best way to teach the Divine Cure is to look at how it relates to our life decisions. For this reason, I will be inviting you to confront your self-limiting and self-destructive patterns and contrast them to the patterns of spirit-filled people who have come to live out their faith, hope, and love.

First, let's consider what each of the three elements is and what it can do for us on our journey.

FAITH

Faith is the theological virtue by which we freely commit our entire lives to God, who invites us to believe in him by stirring our hearts toward him in various ways. Although faith is a *decision* of the will to believe, real faith is not blind. We can't get it on our own. While faith resides beyond the reaches of our intelligence, it is not irrational. It is, rather, a generous response to God, who reveals himself in differing degrees and in different ways based on our unique and limited spiritual sensitivity and openness to him.

God reveals himself to us even when we are at first unaware that it is he. He is revealing himself when we stand in awe of the grandeur of a setting sun, for example, or contemplate our own small stature in relation to a vast, star-speckled night. He is revealing himself when we hold our newborn daughter or son in our arms for the first time, when we reflect on the marvel and mystery of humankind, when prayer is answered, when a soul mate comes unexpectedly into our lives.

As stated above, *faith heals our intellect*. It does this by allowing our mind to grasp the supernatural level of reality that is just as true as the physical properties we can discover through our five senses.

Scripture reminds us of the nature and importance of faith:

Now faith is being sure of what we hope for and certain of what we do not see. (Heb. 11:1, NIV)

Take the shield of faith, with which you will be able to quench all the flaming arrows of the evil one. (Eph. 6:16, NRSV)

But as foundational as faith is for our journey, when it is deprived of hope and love (or charity), faith will die, and so will our spirit-filled living.

HOPE

Hope is the theological virtue by which we desire and count on the blessings of God in our lives, no matter the trial of the moment. The hopeful person is not necessarily an optimist. Optimism and pessimism are emotional states that can come and go without asking our permission. Hope is different. The hopeful person has an eminently positive perspective on life because she knows that an all-loving and all-powerful God is by her side, on her side, and in control—*if* she decides to let him be God for her.

We have said that *faith heals our intellect* by allowing us to grasp spiritual realities. *Hope,* on the other hand, *heals our memory* and allows us to move forward in confidence, despite our remembering our own many failings of the past, and how others have failed us in the past, because we know that God is all-powerful, is all-loving, and will be faithful to his promises. A couple verses from scripture that illustrate this follow:

> Let us hold fast to the confession of our hope without wavering, for he who has promised is faithful. (Heb. 10:23, NRSV)

> Rejoice in your hope, be patient in suffering, persevere in prayer. (Rom. 12:12, NRSV)

As in the case of faith alone, with only faith and hope we don't yet have the complete divine package for spiritual maturity; we still need love.

LOVE

The third leg of the Divine Cure is love. Love is the theological virtue by which we give ourselves to God above all things and to our neighbor as ourselves. Perhaps you have heard non-Christians express their admiration for Jesus as a moral teacher. Specifically, in the arena of world religions, Jesus's teachings stand out for what we call the "New Commandment" of love, in which we are called to "love one another as [Jesus has] loved you," including forgiving even our enemies. I've always found the concept of love as a *new* commandment rather odd. If God is outside of time, and if love is so important, why did he allow thousands of years to go by without explaining to his creatures what life was all about? Why did he give Moses one set of laws and then, hundreds of years later, give *the* law? Jesus's words give us a clue:

> This is my commandment, that you love one another as I have loved you. Greater love has no man than this, that a man lay down his life for his friends. (John 15:12–13, RSV)

It's as if God knew we would never understand a commandment of selfless love unless and until we saw him love us perfectly first in a world of ghastly imperfection. The "Old Law" was a period of preparation for the "New Law." The New Law, then, doesn't *replace* the Old Law—the Ten Commandments, for example. God became man in the person of Jesus of Nazareth and loved us "to the end" by offering his life up as our ransom. He took our sins upon his back and presented his innocence to his Father in our place, even as his creatures continued to reject him by nailing him to the cross. When Jesus asks us to love our enemies, he does so having loved us first—fallible humans who have made ourselves "enemies" of God through Adam's and Eve's rejection of God's love, through our crucifixion of him, and through our own sin today.

Because the word *love* has so many connotations, let's remember how the apostle Paul described it for us:

> Love is patient and kind; love is not jealous or boastful; it is not arrogant or rude. Love does not insist on its own way; it is not irritable or resentful; it does not rejoice at wrong, but rejoices in the right. Love bears all things, believes all things, hopes all things, endures all things. (1 Cor. 13:4–7, RSV)

"If I . . . have not love," clarifies Paul, "I am nothing" (13:2). "If I . . . have not love, I gain nothing" (13:3). And still more clearly, "So faith, hope, love abide, these three; but the greatest of these is love" (13:13).

We said that *faith heals our intellect* and *hope heals our memory*. Similarly, we can say that *love heals our will* by ordering our interests and actions toward giving ourselves to God and others, for their own sake.

THE HEALING OF our mind, memory, and will through the Divine Cure of faith, hope, and love is not magical, but it is miraculous. It requires our cooperation, but the results in our soul cannot be explained by brute human force, desire, or virtue. The Faith-Hope-Love Cure is God stepping in and incorporating us into his divine life, where we discover who we are today—in all of our human misery—and who God created us to be—in all of our potential glory. This kind of spirit-filled living is spiritual freedom. It is the difference between trembling before our God as slaves or mercenaries trying to make do in a crazy world, and standing alongside our loving Father as sons and daughters who have been created by love, redeemed by love, and who are now living in his loving embrace.

The next step of our journey from self-help to God's help and toward spirit-filled living is specifying where and how God wants us to help ourselves and, on the other hand, where and how we need to let go and let him work in us.

For the Divine Cure to take root in our hearts and in our daily lives, we have to show God that we want him to act. God never forces us to make this decision. The theological truth that grace builds on nature without destroying it assumes that if an unhealthy nature (yours or mine) doesn't want to change, grace will respectfully leave us to our own self-destructive devices. God is not in the business of coercion, but rather conversion!

CHAPTER 5

Living Faith

I f you have never known a spirit-filled person and never felt the lasting joy of the Spirit in your life, you may still have some doubt about your potential for such radical transformation. I realize I have not yet proved that such a quest for happiness is realistic. From the beginning of recorded history, thinkers have identified happiness as humankind's destination and have parsed its meaning. They have written many thousands of volumes and composed countless scores and ballads about the philosophy of happiness.

I am tempted to add my two cents to such musings, for I do find some (probably selfish) pleasure in philosophizing about ideals, while avoiding the harder question of how to attain them. When it comes to the pursuit of happiness, it's easiest to talk in philosophical riddles. But I know that this raw intellectual exercise would be unaccomplished, to start, and would serve only the purpose of procrastinating, holding you and me up from getting to the existential place we must go. Rather than prove the concept of beatitude—the ultimate happiness—let's go there and see it up close.

This place we will go is a playing field of great consequence. Seen in another light, it is the intersection where we can lend intellect, memory, and will to the transformative divine powers of faith, hope, and love. It is where the Divine Cure takes hold and we become spirit-filled.

I'm assuming that by now we have already begun to make straight the path, as described in an earlier chapter. The first time we work through those steps, if we do it with courage and humility, it hurts deeply. We wince in pain because we are leaving a comfort zone of denial and self-restriction that we have built up over many years. We want to cry when we see on paper or share with a trustworthy friend the high-def picture of the faults, sins, and addictions we have identified, with God's grace.

There is always a first time to make straight the path, but we can never let that process go. Every day is a new day to start over and to win just that day. Our preparations for grace will eventually become second nature, but the first day that we take a straight path for granted is the last day of growth. A straight path forged by spiritual humility, and groomed routinely over the weeks and years, is the foundation of the Divine Cure, which begins with faith.

FEELING THE PRESENCE OF GOD IN OUR "MESSY MOMENTS"

Much has been *said* of faith. Probably too much. *Talking* about faith is very different than *spreading it by living it*. Admittedly, I speak of faith in most every sermon, certainly in every counseling session, and in many chance encounters. I speak of faith in lots of ways, with plenty of metaphors and examples to illuminate this marvelous gift. But words always come up short. We don't "understand" faith; we "get it." "Getting" faith, however, is usually sparked by understanding certain things about it. We say, for example, that faith lifts us up. It lifts our minds and hearts to believe in God and in his ways without our needing scientific, material proof. Faith is our human way of saying yes to divine revelation—God making himself known to us.

But at the end of the day, among believers and unbelievers alike, most people's minds, when freed from the frets of business affairs, are on soccer practice, dirty diapers, and unpaid bills. For both the believer and the nonbeliever, the human condition is fixed for the most part on mundane things. And for as much as we may wish to lift our eyes off the earth and up to the things of God, common sense tells us that earthly survival and success require keeping our feet firmly planted on planet earth and our eyes focused earthward.

This unavoidable reality should give us confidence that God's idea of faith-filled living has nothing to do with living in the clouds. He put us on earth and told us to "subdue" it (Gen. 1:28, rsv). There should be no wonder, then, that we feel rather earthy as we go about placing our own positive mark on this earth, according to God's plans—that is, subduing it. Even my daily duties that are so centered on spirituality—preparing talks, leading staff meetings, making hospital visits, preaching, praying—are very human affairs. No matter how spiritual the activity at hand may be, we have to show up on time, assess the situation, and get to work, none of which is easy.

This is not to say we can throw in the towel on living immersed in faith. Just the opposite! We need to throw in the towel on what so many of us have thought faith to be, or have acted as if it were—either a one-time profession of belief in God or our response to an impossible command of God to always think and act like angels, to spurn the world and float six inches off the ground.

The Divine Cure that begins with *living faith* is very different than either of those two cultural misconceptions. It is a lifestyle of living our "messy moments" in the presence of God. It is an awareness of our vocation as cocreators with God of our little corner of his kingdom. It is intentional living with and among ordinary and routine things.

Living faith is knowing experientially, in my bones, who I am as a beloved child of God with a great mission to fulfill on earth; it is being aware of who I am called to be, and being confident in the inestimable value of what I am doing right now, right here, as a Junior Partner of the Holy Spirit, engaged in redemption. It is jumping enthusiastically into making history, even if what I might accomplish, if all goes well, is so small that nobody will even notice.

Living faith is not a mind game. It is not a mere mental exercise of faithfulness to life's priorities under a divine guilt trip. Philosophers have belabored the point, and generally agree that "action" follows "being," and that certain types of action point to certain qualities of being. If that is so, then consciousness of having been made out of love, and in the image and likeness of God—that is, awareness of who we are before God—enables us for action of an otherworldly, divine quality.

Living faith is a lifestyle remedy to the shallowness that sucks us dry of supernatural vision and life. Shallowness takes many different forms, but in its essence it is a horizontal, two-dimensional view of our lives and others. Shallowness is horizontal because it ignores in practice our "vertical" connection with God. It is two-dimensional because it seduces us to relate to people for what they look like, what they do for a living, whom they know, and—worst of all—what they can do for us.

Although there is a wide range of spiritual sensitivity levels, the good news is that nobody is *born* shallow; we arrive on this earth with inner antennae pointing us toward deep things. A child's soul and personality are marked indelibly toward goodness, not by the hip—or not-so-hip—color of her nursery, not by the size of her parents' second home, and not even by her early educational opportunities. A child is formed most definitively by deep things, beginning with the amount of love she experiences around her. It is her parents' early caresses, whispers, spiritual education, and loving choices that forge for her a deep and solid foundation. Do we need any other proof of being spiritual beings than watching a child grow and a personality blossom?

Children are deep because in their innocence they are pure, and purity is inherently deep. Deep souls are sensitive to things of lasting importance. Shallow souls don't see beyond the surface.

Last week I received a note that made my heart jump and tears well up in my eyes. I couldn't believe what I was reading. It was from a young girl about ten years old, who was in a religion class I had been offering to a few families. She wrote just one line: "I can't wait to go to church on Sunday." This was Tuesday, and this ten-year-old girl was looking forward to church on Sunday?! I forwarded the note to her mom, first of all to make sure she knew her daughter had found my e-mail address and had written to me, but also so she could see the spiritual depth of her daughter, who usually acted as if she wasn't paying attention in class. Her mother replied, "Thank you. Yes, I gave Michelle your address. P.S. Every night before going to sleep, she reads to me from the prayer book you gave her. Thank you."

. . .

As we grow up, we make choices that either mature or dampen our sensitivity to supernatural realities and to what's important in life. Naturally we lose some innocence—that's part of life—but we don't have to lose the purity and depth of our soul. And even if we lose those, as long as we have breath they are within our reach, ready to be renewed by our work and God's help.

Just as a wine connoisseur trains his palate to identify and appreciate quality by tasting quality products, so the person of fledgling faith becomes deeper, believes more deeply, through his increasing contact with God. Nobody becomes an expert connoisseur by drinking wine-in-a-box. And no soul grows more spiritual without breaking through the surface of appearance and through visible realities by the *exercise* of faith.

Living faith is possible once we have tasted God through faith in sapling form (through human love or through contact with the beauty of his creation, for example) and have made it grow by going back to connect with God more directly, again and again, in quiet prayer. The most powerful and rapid growth in prayer occurs when we form the habit of living the moment *in his presence* and doing our daily duties with perfection out of love for him.

Fostering living faith by striving for absolute perfection is impossible if we measure the value of our actions by human standards: "How much have I done today?" "Do people I respect and love appreciate my work?" "Could I have performed better if I had known more?"

If, on the other hand, we measure the value of our actions by God's standards, we ask questions of another sort: "Did I act righteously?" "Were my intentions good?" "Did I do my best?" "Have I apologized if I've made a mistake and caused others to suffer?"

Overcoming shallowness requires living in the present. Today you find in many self-help books a call to "presence," "awareness," or "consciousness." We make a mistake if we dismiss this invitation as New Age drivel. These are words that recognize the fact that we waste much of our energy and suffer uselessly by focusing on what we wish the past had been or what the future could be. Doing so, we fail to live the moment in its fullness. Training our mind to live the moment without distraction, as many of these authors teach, is a very healthy thing; it's a great start.

But living faith is much more than mere mind control or focus. The man or woman of living faith knows and experiences why this present moment is worth living fully. And as a result, that person lives the moment differently, more profoundly, more gratefully, and with transforming intentionality.

Living in God's presence starts with, and continues with, our steps in the Make Straight the Path process. For before we can bask in living faith, in God's garden of peace and love found in a purified soul, we must clear the brush and uproot the weeds of our own sinfulness. Along the way of such conversion we can begin to cultivate seeds of presence. We can talk to God as we wash the dishes, hire an employee, drive to the next client, or carry on a heated phone conversation. Talking to God doesn't have to involve full sentences or full thoughts. It is a sometimes conscious and sometimes subconscious choice to live in accordance with our identity as loved children of God and to stay connected with him on a spiritual level.

Have you ever watched an elderly couple reading the morning newspaper together at a local coffee shop? Even if most of the time they don't talk to each other, you can tell both are enjoying the other's presence. Once in a while one may point out a headline or a picture, but most of the time they're doing their own thing, reading their own section of the paper, while very much doing it *together*. How different our day can be when we do our own ordinary tasks in the presence of God, pointing things out to him, asking for his guidance, thanking him, praising him.

As noted in the previous chapter, living faith effects a healing of our intellect. Because we are weak, mortal, and sinful human beings, our intellect is limited by design and wounded by sin. If we depend on our intellect to give us a full grasp of reality, we will miss the mark. Just as the brain takes in data from our senses, processes it, and comes to a judgment, so our spiritual soul takes in data, processes it, and accepts, through faith, the supernatural truth it has encountered.

COLLABORATING IN THE WORK OF FAITH

By now it should be clear, after learning how we can become Junior Partners with the Holy Spirit and working toward making straight the path, that no part of the Divine Cure happens without some human collaboration. The transformative power of faith to bring us from shallowness to living faith is all about God healing our intellect. Ironically, this healing can happen only if we choose (with our intellect!) to allow God to enlighten our intellect with the gift of faith, aware that faith is never forced upon us and must be accepted as a free gift.

All of us who have at one point or another made an act of faith in God, in the face of temptations to disbelieve or despair, know that faith doesn't come easily. There is a letting go involved. We let go of pride. We let go of fear. We let go of our desire for control. We invite Jesus to take the reins. That may be easy for the meek and humble—or easier, at least—but it is awfully unpleasant for the rest of us. If one act of faith is laborious, then we can expect acquiring the habit of living faith—basking in faith continuously as believing children of God, charging forward while always giving the reins to Jesus—to be a program in patient work.

Thinking through what this work might entail takes us back to the third and fourth steps in our Make Straight the Path process: (3) Turn your will over to God's care and live trusting that he can make you whole; (4) begin to live the New Commandment: "Love one another as I have loved you."

In these steps there is plenty of room for self-help—exercising our will in virtue and prayer. Let us never forget, however, that this self-help will have eternal value only when we are consistently entrusting this spiritual work to the Lord.

As a priest I am not miraculously exempt from this work. It took a heart-wrenching act of faith to follow God's call to leave behind my dreams of business, politics, marriage, and family and enter the seminary at the age of twenty-one. The choices for or against faith that I've had to make since then, over these last seventeen years, have been challenging. In some cases, I was up to the challenge. In many others I failed. By the grace of God, I am still here and still trying every day.

Over the last three years my faith has been tested more than during any other period of my life. One night, with no warning and with no premonition, I received news that the man who had founded my religious congregation and had stood at its helm for sixty years, a man whom I had come to know personally and love deeply and whom I looked up to as my model for how to follow Jesus, was in fact a very different person than I had thought. He had allowed me and many others to see one side of his life—the side filled with generous good works, organizational genius, gentleness, kindness, and compassion, and at least a façade of spiritual depth I had never witnessed in anyone else. From him personally I received nothing but goodness, and not once did I doubt that my experience of him was not the same as everyone else's. Everything he allowed me to see testified that it must be so: he must be a spirit-filled, faithful man.

As the days and months passed after the initial news of his fraud, more and more information surfaced, exposing many other sides of his life—aspects I had never seen and never would have imagined could coexist in any single person, much less him. Leaving aside any judgment of his personal culpability (for only God knows a person's heart), what I do know is that my first spiritual father—the one who invited me to join the religious congregation he founded (a religious order I have now left) and who encouraged me along the way for many years, was in fact a serial pedophile, plagiarist, legal impostor, mostly absent father of several illegitimate children, and manipulator of biblical proportions. The Vatican ultimately described him as being "devoid of any religious sentiment."

The man who for years taught me to believe in Jesus as the way, the truth, and the life was secretly entangled in a web of activity as antithetical to Jesus's teachings as one could imagine.

As I have struggled with these revelations, I can only imagine what the direct victims of his sexual and psychological abuse have had to suffer before me, and surely still suffer today. My heart bleeds for them. I am sorry for not having believed them earlier and for being part of the large crowd of this man's followers who assumed, and indeed proclaimed, that the victims were the villains.

Some of my friends and colleagues feel betrayed— understandably and perhaps healthily so—having learned of this man's transgressions. They gave many of the best years of their lives to collaborate in his mission. Others were benefactors and gave large sums of money, and still others were men and women of great repute who put their good name on the line by defending him against his accusers based on what they thought to be true.

I cannot tell this story without being overwhelmed by grief. Had I known as an idealistic young man of twenty-one that saying yes to God would mean leaving all to follow in the footsteps of a man some psychologists would later call a psychopath and a sociopath, I surely would have been overwhelmed by the prospect of what would come my way. I would instead have chosen suburbia and a white picket fence. I'm glad I didn't see it coming, for I'm glad I am where I am. And now, several years into this drama, I can say with confidence that I believe God did call me to embark on what turned out to be a very crooked path, and I am grateful he gave me the grace to say yes.

I tell you my story because I can hardly invite you into my world of spirituality, and particularly into forming living faith, without opening my heart to you and showing you how and why my soul moves as it does today.

This event shook me to the core, and hopefully it will shake me to the core until the day I die. I say this because in this spiritual earthquake, I have found new ways of living faith, no longer as an apparently perfect soldier with only hidden battle scars, but rather as a friend of Jesus who has been beaten and bloodied in public with him.

I don't know why, but unlike some people much holier than I am, I don't feel the least amount of bitterness toward this man. I hold not an ounce of anger in my heart toward him. If he showed up at my door today, I would feel only mercy toward him and gratitude to God for how he blessed me through this man—and in spite of him too. Admittedly, my attitude has less to do with virtue and more to do with my partial and subjective personal experience of his life. Perhaps it's due also to my own personality, for everyone experiences and deals with things in a unique way—a sacrosanct principle to be remembered when we encounter human suffering. But this doesn't mean I came through unscathed. While others in similar shoes understandably are beaten up by feelings of betrayal and by memories of the past, my spiritual challenge after the shock has been in discerning what faith says to me about moving forward. Working toward living faith in my new circumstances has been a challenge and also a great source of joy. Reminding myself day in and day out of who I am as a son of God, and of Jesus's relentless and creative plan to draw me closer to himself, is the ultimate context-builder in tragedy. My faith in God, though rattled, assures me of the straight and narrow road he has made for me. My road now is about getting back to the basics of living faith. I am in new circumstances, no doubt, but God's love for me has not changed one bit, and my faith is in *him,* not in human beings, and not in institution.

When I look back at the steps involved in the Make Straight the Path process—a process I so ardently believe in—I know, in this period of my life, that I have particular work to do in steps 3 and 4, restated above: renewing my belief that Jesus can make me and others whole, and deciding once again to turn my will and life over to him and to live the New Commandment of love of neighbor, as he loved us. Both of these truths fly in the face of self-pity. My living faith—embodied as me when I'm living the moment aware of who I am and who I'm called to be—has no room for pity parties. It's so full of awareness of our loving God that it doesn't dwell on things it cannot reverse or make disappear. Our living faith is powerful because it is more about God and his call in and through my life to live for him and for others than it is about me and my past.

Thomas Merton, a well-known monk and author of contemporary Christian mysticism, was a profoundly spiritual soul who had more than his fair share of suffering and confusion. In a particularly difficult period of his life he penned the following prayer. I love it for its transparency. It shows real faith, alive and well in a human soul, even as Merton was searching for God's will for him.

> *My Lord God, I have no idea where I am going.*
>
> *I do not see the road ahead of me, I cannot know for certain where it will end. Nor do I really know myself, and the fact that I think I am following Your will does not mean that I am actually doing so. But I believe that the desire to please You does in fact please You. And I hope I have that desire in all that I am doing. I hope that I will never do anything apart from that desire to please You. And I know that if I do this, you will lead me by the right road, though I may know nothing about it. Therefore I will trust You always though I may seem to be lost and in the shadow of death. I will not fear, for You are ever with me, and You will never leave me to face my perils alone.*
>
> —from *Thoughts in Solitude*, Thomas Merton

Do you see how the process of making straight the path truly makes way for the Lord? On the one hand, it points us to spiritual principles. On the other hand, it keeps us from overspiritualizing our earthly journey. Sometimes we *say* we want more faith, but unless we're willing to give a signal to God to come in and transform our heart, deep down we don't *really* want it. If I haven't recognized my own misery, my need for God, and if I haven't turned over the reins of my life to him, with willingness to make amends for my previous errors, I am continuously walking this earth with a sign on top of my head, directed toward the heavens—"God, stay away!"

We erect our "I don't want your help" signs for various reasons. I know an elderly woman who owns a stunning three-bedroom unit in an ocean-front condominium with a large terrace overlooking the surf. Although money is not a factor for her, the unit is in terrible shape. The very apartment that would be the object of envy of all her neighbors is a monument to her own fear of change. She hates her old, leaky windows, but she can't stand to think of a contractor ripping them out. Her appliances don't work, but getting new ones would mean "all that hassle of moving things in and out of the apartment." That's how we can be with God: we know that he should be a bigger part of our lives, but we fear the discomfort of doing our part.

The transition from *our* work of path-straightening to *God's* work of instilling in us living faith is not linear. We never graduate from self-help to God's help, for the two are intertwined and inseparable by divine design. We never forge such perfect habits of self-discipline that we can rest on our laurels and float on clouds, waiting for God to do his part. Living faith is qualitatively different and better than the practice of human virtue, but it will always be sustained by our willingness and action to prepare our nature for the grace of the moment and for the boatloads of grace God has in store for us.

STEPPING INTO LIVING FAITH WITH A "YES"

We've said that living faith is a lifestyle remedy to shallowness. How do we get there? "Lifestyle" implies a consistent pattern of thought and action, and this, I assure you, is the only way faith will transform us. Faith as a lifestyle is the only way we become spirit-filled. But faith's transformative power does not come as the natural effect of repeated action, as in the case of the formation of human virtue. (If I jump out of bed every morning when the alarm goes off, it usually becomes easier to do so with time—that's human virtue.) Faith is infused in our soul by the direct action of God in response to the signals we give him that indeed we want his gift. If we give him repeated signals, and he in turn repeatedly gives us more faith, with time we begin to think and act in accordance with our new and deeper understanding of reality. Believing in God becomes thinking with God and participating in his life and work.

Growing up, I always thought my parents were basically perfect. In our home, "Because I said so!" coming from Mom or Dad, especially Dad, was good enough reason to end any dispute with them. I always knew they couldn't be wrong because they were the parents (although I came to realize, as an all-knowing adolescent, that they were *usually* wrong!). As the seven of us kids have gotten older and moved out of the house, we've had a lot of fun going back and analyzing our upbringing. At family gatherings it's not uncommon for us to laugh to the point of hysteria as we recall one or another story of how we got around Mom's and Dad's watchful eyes. Mom and Dad are astonished now with what we got away with and are surprisingly great sports, when only a few years back none of our tales would have been a laughing matter, I assure you!

More interesting still than recalling our childhood adventures has been growing into an adult relationship with Mom and Dad. Perhaps in part because I am the priest in the family, but mostly because my parents are increasingly open with everyone about their spiritual walk, I have learned more about my parents over the last five years than in the previous thirty-two. The more I know about them, including their imperfect pasts and the behind-the-scenes story of their relationship and their teamwork in raising us, the more I respect and adore them and try to learn from them. When I have a tough pastoral case, wrestle with a personal problem, am preparing to speak to a group, or am writing a book, I often seek their advice. Regarding living faith in action, both of them have passed on to me some amazing wisdom.

Mom likes to write her thoughts down, usually at some ungodly hour in the morning when she can't sleep or just wants to take advantage of the quiet. When talking about what helps her live faith as a lifestyle, Mom always goes back to the importance of knowing who we are before God and what makes us wonderful, as the foundation for everything else. Her living faith is remarkably strong because she has whittled away the false conceptions of her self-worth. She tells me that this did not come overnight. But what she believes and lives now is remarkable. Look at this letter I received from her this week:

> *I often define my role in life as being a mother to my children, a wife to my husband, a grandmother, a social worker, a friend, a sister to Ralph and to wonderful Mary Ellen and Therese and Loretta and to Andrew, a daughter of Ralph and Mary, a Catholic, a born-again believer, and a member of this or that group, all of which I love. My life is full of these relationships. But do you know what? I am very precious to God outside of every one of these important people and groups in my life. My life has meaning and "vocation" just because I have life. If my church fell apart; if I had to move away and I could no longer spend time with my grandchildren; if my children turned out to be failures and turned away from God and from me and their dad; if my brother wasn't Ralph*

Martin or Andrew Martin, and my child wasn't Joy or Joseph or
Father Jonathan or Mary Hope or Christine or Anne Marie or
Bobby; if my husband left me or died; and even if all my friends
decided that I wasn't so nice to be around, and I became friendless
and homeless and alone—my life would still have meaning and
"vocation" just because I have life and I am the daughter of a divine
king. And when I know that, through faith, I also have hope.

What most people learn from life's hard knocks about where *not* to
find happiness can be learned in the positive, especially through what
God has revealed to us in the Bible about who we are. Indeed, the very
first book of the Bible reveals to us who we are and what we are doing
here on earth.

Then the Lord God formed man of dust from the ground, and
breathed into his nostrils the breath of life; and man became a
living being. (Gen. 2:7, RSV)

Then God said, "Let us make man in our image, according to
our likeness; and let them have dominion over the fish of the
sea and over the birds of the air, and over the cattle, and over
all the earth." (Gen. 1:26, RSV)

We learn several things about ourselves from these complementary
accounts of God's creation of humanity. First, that men and women are
physical, material beings. We have been formed "from the dust of the
ground," like every other creature. In other words, we are not angels!
We need food, water, sleep, and sunlight. We have real needs and
desires, and we can experience real pain and pleasure because of the

bodies God has given us. And all of this is good! Our bodies are good. Our sexuality is good. Our love for food is good. Our physicality was given to us by God and should not be shunned; he willed it all from the beginning. But we also learn from these passages that we are spiritual beings: God "breathed into [our] nostrils the breath of life." He didn't do this to the trees or to any other animal. God's special gift to us is a soul enlivened by his own Spirit. In the second creation account quoted above, the authors of Genesis tell us what this divine sharing of the Spirit means. Speaking in the plural, God (the three persons of the Trinity—Father, Son, and Holy Spirit) says, "Let us make man [and woman] in our image, according to our likeness." Together with the announcement of the incarnation of Jesus and the passion story, this must be among the most important lines of the Bible. God is telling us he loved us so much that he made us like him! The Trinity breathed into us their Spirit, and we became "according to their likeness."

Does it not make sense, then, that to the degree we reject God's place in our life, we are rejecting our true nature? It is for this reason that we find bits of happiness in lots of God's creatures, for they are in some way participants in his nature too, but ultimate happiness can be found only in uniting ourselves with him and his will for us. This union with God happens through faith, beginning with a decision to let him into our lives, then progressing to living faith, and coming to completion in heaven, where every tear will be wiped away.

Below is the second half of the letter my Mom sent to me. It's her story of a search for meaning and her first act of faith:

> *I like to talk about "finding meaning" in life, because throughout my life I have struggled with this. And I think that all of us do. I remember in high school feeling the "darkness" and*

looking for "meaning" outside of the fun and games that were very much a part of my life back then. I realize now that some of this darkness was just my hormones wreaking havoc on my psyche during my menstrual periods! But back then we didn't really talk about things like that, and I didn't know anything about how crabby and anxious women can feel at those times. I thought it was just me, unholy Sharon. But nonetheless, even the darkness and the yearning for meaning led me to pursue the "something more" that eventually led me to giving my life to Christ.

I went to Salve Regina University in Newport, Rhode Island. It's in the town where Jackie and President Kennedy had their summer home. Large mansions, cliffs overlooking the inlet to the ocean—it was quite nice. (My dad won the Irish Sweepstakes, third place, and the money paid for our college education.) At exam time I would study on those cliffs. I did my senior thesis on the officer candidates at the Officer Candidate School (three hundred new good-looking men arriving in town every three months!). It was the "good life." But right in the midst of all this "good life," depression found my doorstep again. I was discovering that although I was a Catholic and went to Mass on Sundays and even weekdays, my life didn't look very different from some of the atheists that I was dating.

What difference did Christ make in my life? What meaning did my life have? I felt like I was being a hypocrite. With difficulty, I made a decision to stop going to church and started searching for answers.

Nearing the end of my junior year of college, as I was still searching and my life was taking paths I really didn't want to go down, I received a letter from my brother Ralph—and just in the nick of time! Mind you, this is the first letter that he ever wrote me. In grammar school I used to deliver notes to him from a girl who was crazy about him. But in this historic note he told me how he had been struggling in his faith and looking for answers and that he had found what he was looking for. He had found Jesus. He wanted me to know Jesus too, and he asked if I would like to spend the summer in Michigan working with the Mexican migrants and living close by.

What a great summer job! Not only was it wonderful working with people who could use my help, but I could try out my Spanish. During that summer I worked alongside a group of young people who were so very happy. I hadn't seen happiness like this in fancy Newport. I wanted what they had. A young seminarian began reading the Bible to me during our time off, and I started sitting in the back of the church during services. One day Ralph led me up a small hill. We sat and talked, and he asked me if I would like to give my whole life to Christ.

Unanswered questions flew through my mind, but I felt assured that in time these would be answered. At that moment, I surrendered my life to Christ. Amazing grace, how sweet it is! I went to confession, turned away from my sins, and called the man I'd been dating back in Newport and told him that I couldn't see him anymore. He was a great guy, but our paths no longer were the same. Life had changed in a heartbeat, and it was a change that has lasted for forty-two years—a lifetime. Meaning in my life was now oozing out of every step I took. I was walking with the Holy Spirit!

My mom is certainly a person of great spirit-filled living. On rare occasions I've seen her yell or cry, to be sure, and we've disagreed on more than a handful of things. (Our areas of disagreement— often in discussions of right and wrong—are probably one of the best signs that she's spirit-filled!) She will tell you that her act of faith forty-two years ago, though monumental and life-changing, didn't make all of her problems disappear. It didn't make her feel good changing the diapers of seven kids or pay the bills for her. Her faith didn't make my dad tell her he loved her every time he saw her, as she may have liked. And my hunch is there have been times when she's had to hold tight to a dry faith, times when the meaning and joy of life eluded her.

With time we learn that there is nothing surprising about faith struggles. Faith very rarely heals our intellect in one big swoop, such that we think, act, and even feel with the heart of God all of a sudden. Living faith takes time, sweat, and sometimes blood to take hold, for it is a culmination of lots of little healings. Nevertheless, the long process of acquiring living faith rarely takes place at all if it doesn't start off with a single moment (or series of moments) of a radical and definitive acceptance of God in our life. You've probably heard people refer to themselves as "cradle Catholics" or "cradle Christians." By that they mean they were raised with faith, and that's a blessing for sure. But I've never met a person of deep, spirit-filled living who hasn't at one or another time in his or her life made a serious, adult decision to live for and under God. Sometimes the decision is dramatic, like my mother's; other times it's lived without any spiritual fireworks at all. God is creative, and he meets us where we are and according to our own sensibilities, preferences, and personalities.

What's the difference between the decision we made in step three of the Make Straight the Path journey, which involved turning our heart and will over to God's care and trusting him to make us whole, and this first yes to God in living faith? It's the difference between saying yes to the idea of marriage and saying yes to the man you love who is on one knee with a ring in his hand. It's the difference between an intellectual belief in a higher power and an experiential consent to a God who loves you intimately and who has a wonderful plan for you going forward. Both are important. The first leads to the latter, which is a very special gift—a gift worth asking for!

Speaking of adult decisions of faith, do you remember Jim and Samantha, from chapter 2? He was a compulsive liar, as you may recall, which understandably troubled Samantha as the couple became seriously involved. Eventually they made the decision to separate until Jim got things under control. This was at Jim's initiative, and his intention was as sincere as could be. Through the grace of God he made a searching and fearless moral inventory of his life. He accepted that his habit of lying had started way before meeting Samantha and that the tension between them was not due to any "hypersensitivity" on her part. With help, he came to understand his lying as a consequence of deep-seated vanity—an oversized vanity that flowed from insecurity, which in turn was rooted in his woefully low estimation of self-worth, probably brought on by the constant disapproval and abandonment he'd felt from his dad as a youngster. With more human help and lots of God's participation (working overtime and discreetly), Jim reached the point at which he accepted his powerlessness to stop lying. This realization led him to a very, very low point. For Jim, powerlessness was hopelessness, which for all of us has a way of translating quickly into "Life's not worth living." Unless, of course, there is a higher power that can and will intervene and empower us! Jim already believed in God, but his challenge was to leave behind shallowness, where vanity and insecurity held him hostage, and enter into the adventure of living faith where he could rest, with all of his imperfections, in the heart of God.

To do this Jim needed first to do some more work to make straight the path of the Lord. Particularly, he needed to renew his belief that God could make him whole and decide once again to turn his will and life over to God and to live the New Commandment of love of God and neighbor above all else.

If these two steps—the third and fourth—seem to be showing up a lot, that's because they're lifetime projects. They are at the beginning, middle, and end of the Faith-Hope-Love Cure. I'm living proof of that. If you remember, when I told you the story of my most recent challenge in faith, I ended by recognizing that these steps are precisely the human foundation of the spiritual work I have in front of me today. Even after all of these years of studying, teaching, and trying to live my faith, the ideal of living faith calls me back to simple honesty and humility before God, and to the exercise of my will to make straight the path.

Jim's entrance into living faith redefined my expectations of the grace of God. As much as he'd always liked his faith and his church community, Jim's commitment to God was rather shallow, a fact he would admit readily. His identification with his Christian faith was mostly cultural and social; it was the faith of his parents, who were quite proud of him for still practicing it even in his young adult years in the secular setting of New York City. Much like Pascal, with his famous wager on God's existence, Jim was making the safe bet that Jesus was who he claimed to be, knowing he had little to lose if he was wrong, and heaven to gain if he was right. Even after Jim, prompted by his relationship crisis, began his sincere work to make straight the path,

Jesus had very little to do with Jim's life in New York City. Jim's goal was simply to get himself back on track with good living, and he knew that a higher power should probably be in the mix.

This openness to God was just enough for Jim to accept an invitation to go on a weekend retreat on Long Island. The retreat was mostly silent, but the retreatants had time to speak privately with the director. The director, after conversation with Jim, wisely encouraged him to pray privately for the gift of faith and to bring this intention to the general prayer meeting that would be held the last night of the retreat. As the director and the other retreatants prayed over Jim for the gift of faith during that final prayer meeting, Jim felt a great sense of peace and serenity entering into his soul. Nothing drastic happened to him, but he knew from that moment on that Jesus was real, that Jesus was his friend and Savior, and that he wanted to live the rest of his life for God.

Have you ever asked God to enter your soul in that way? Now may be as good a time as any. If this is your time, fold your hands, close your eyes, and then relax your body by taking in five deep breaths, lifting your shoulders up as you inhale and letting them drop slowly as you exhale. Now, in your own words, speak to Jesus. Don't ask him for anything other than the gift of knowing him and entering into a personal relationship with him, as your friend, Lord, and Redeemer.

Because God respects us so much, because he never forces his grace upon us, it is only by our inviting him to be the guest of our soul that we can begin our Junior Partner work in the Faith-Hope-Love Cure.

Even if you have invited God into your life many times, it is a wonderful exercise in faith and humility to repeat it regularly.

• • •

WHEN JIM CAME back from the retreat and shared with me his experience, I knew it was the real deal. Up to that point all of Jim's work of self-improvement had been about him and Samantha. He wanted to fix himself because it was the only way for him to win back Samantha. He had convinced himself he needed Samantha to be happy—and besides, even if she didn't work out, he would need to get himself in shape for whomever he would date next! He couldn't stand the shame of his screwed-up way of operating. In this postre-treat conversation, Jim mentioned Samantha only once. And even the tone with which he uttered her name was different now, more loving and certainly more humble. It was now about her, not him. His ex-perience of God's presence and love had catapulted him onto another level of seeing the same old circumstances and relationships. Over the period of one weekend, and especially in those short moments of prayer, Jim's intellect and heart were opened to a new realm of real-ity—grace—where belief in God is transformed from cultural mores into existential certainty.

MATURING THROUGH PRAYER AND SACRIFICE

The first, second, and thousandth yes to God—as I've just de-scribed—is just the beginning of forging living faith. Like a sculptor who strikes lightly with his chisel, day in and day out, with the goal of even-tually revealing the figure waiting to come forth from the marble block, we enable the healing of our intellect by making a daily decision to live faith, a process that happens slowly and sometimes painfully. There are ups and downs. We lose sight of our goal. Some days we feel spiritual; some days we don't. We have hazy moments in which the concepts of living faith and the spiritual life in general sound like gibberish.

This marsh of mixed emotions we humans inevitably wade through mustn't be misread as a sign we're on the wrong path. In heaven we will love God effortlessly, for we will see him as he really is—our intellect having been healed perfectly—but for now our imperfect faith must guide us. Living by faith is *supposed* to be hard work.

The surest way to fortify faith is through habits of prayer and sacrifice. A regular prayer life and a readiness to sacrifice comfort in pursuit of our mission are the two planks that best bridge the gap between our tendency toward discouragement and God's great plan for us. Prayer and sacrifice together form the bridge. God's grace moves us across that bridge through the Faith-Hope-Love Cure.

A regular prayer life can take many forms. I've met people who can stay in God's presence and converse with him in the soul (that's prayer in its essence) while doing their ordinary tasks. Continuous contact like this should be our goal too. But I've never met anyone who's achieved this sort of continuous contact with God without first setting regular time aside just for prayer and faithfully respecting that time over a long period, usually many years. A regular prayer time requires carving out a slot in our daily schedule to meditate or to contemplate spiritual truths (scripture being our usual source) and then to talk and listen to God as he conforms our mind and heart to himself through grace.

If we don't respect a regular and daily prayer time, we will tend to pray only when we feel spiritual or when we're already in deep trouble that we probably could have avoided if we'd been praying regularly in the first place. If our spiritual growth depends only on feel-good moments or rock-bottom moments—the typical prayer prompts—we will grow very slowly. I have found that my most consequential moments of prayer come on days when I have no desire to pray and nothing major to ask for. Every day that we are faithful to the time we have set aside for prayer, we are sending signals to God that we want him to penetrate our soul. Incidentally, isn't it usually when we don't feel like praying that we most need God to enter?

Below is a simple outline for your prayer time. I offer it to you as a suggestion, especially for beginners. I pray this way every morning. The format is based on steps of traditional Christian meditation. When we don't feel like praying, when we don't feel particularly spiritual or inspired, outlines like this can lead us into God's presence. The art of Christian meditation is a lost treasure, waiting to be rediscovered by Christians of our day. Perhaps you have found helpful the breathing exercises and physical techniques taught in yoga or other Eastern meditation traditions as a way to recover physical and emotional stillness from the frazzled world in which we live. As such, I think these techniques are good. But Christian meditation necessarily takes us further than Eastern meditation: it is an encounter with God, not just our own "center." I believe there are as many good ways to pray as there are people on this earth. If you find a better way for you than what I offer here, use it. This is what works for me:

1. *Get into the place and posture where you are least distracted and most open to the whispers of God.* For some this may be sipping coffee in a favorite lounge chair; for others, kneeling in a church; and for still others, sitting cross-legged on the floor. Test out various venues and postures and see what works best for you. Remember, you're looking not for what is most comfortable necessarily, but rather where and how you can

best hear the whispers of God. At the beginning, most prayer postures will be a bit uncomfortable until you train your mind and body to be at rest.

2. *Place yourself (mind and heart) in the presence of God.* This entails making a simple act of faith that God is near you, with you, in your soul; that he loves you; and that he wants to converse with you today and make you more like him. I generally make this act of faith while simultaneously resting my mind by taking several deep breaths and letting the air out slowly. Direct the act of faith to God himself, in words of your own choosing, along these lines: "God, I love you and believe that you are present with me right now. I place myself in your presence. I'm a bit tired and have a lot on my mind, but I want to dedicate this time to you. Please work in my soul. Help me to hear your whispers." There's no need to rush this first step; it's an important one. Sometimes I find that placing myself in God's presence is a deep prayer in and of itself, because it means shedding all other concerns and trusting in God.

3. *Make a simple act of humility.* Because there is no such thing as egocentric Christian prayer, effective communication with God requires an act of humility: recognizing God for who he is and submitting our mind and heart to him in dialogue. This act of humility can be directed to God in words like these: "Jesus, I thank you for the gift of this time that I'm able to dedicate to dialoguing with you. I cannot save myself. I cannot make sense of my life without you. You are my origin, and you sustain me in every moment. Make me more

humble. Mold my heart to be more open to your whispers. Forgive me for my pride, vanity, and laziness [insert here any specific sins or faults you have on your conscience]. Make me more like you. I love you, Jesus."

4. *Read a few paragraphs (a chapter at most) of a spiritual author whom you trust.* Usually I use the Bible, particularly the Gospels. Read slowly and reflect on the meaning of God's Word. This is not a Bible study or a literary analysis; rather, use your intellect, imagination, and memory—in combination with your reading—to build context and to insert yourself into it. Fill out a Bible story with what might have been going on in the minds of the different personalities, for example. Ask yourself why Jesus might have said this or that. You can even "live the scene" in the shoes of one of the characters involved. The temptation here is to jump to conclusions on your own about what God wants to tell you in the passage. To avoid that trap, allow his lesson to seep into your soul. Sometimes I recognize the lesson clearly by an idea that comes to my mind—an idea that is probably inspired by God. Other times I walk out of prayer without having grasped much of anything of what God may have wanted to say; then, halfway through the day, or the following week, I make a connection to the reading in a surprising way. Prayer is not about learning more things or even getting something out of it for our own good. Prayer is conversing with God and allowing him to transform our mind and heart according to his perfect will and timing. Just as you wouldn't go to a dinner date to get something out of the conversation for your

own self-improvement, in prayer we go just to be with God, to talk to him as a son or daughter talks to loving parents.

5. *After reflecting on the objective input you have received from your spiritual reading, take time to be quiet.* Prayer quiet is not only silencing exterior noise or mental distractions; it is silent listening, but with no pressure to hear. The best way I can describe this prayer quiet is "resting in God." Too often we fill our prayers with our own words. We tell God our problems and ask him to help. The kind of prayer I am suggesting certainly involves pouring out our soul to God and petitioning him for our needs, but it is first of all dialogue that begins with quieting our being.

6. *Now enter into conversation with God.* Several times now, I have referred to prayer as conversation with God, but how is this accomplished? The prayer quiet established in the previous step is the prelude to intimate dialogue. I usually allow God to initiate the dialogue. Sometimes, in the midst of my prayer quiet, I sense a very clear movement of my heart to thank God for something. Other times I feel God's presence, and my dialogue becomes a wordless acceptance of him. More often than I would like, the quiet leads to acknowledgment of selfishness or some other sin in my life. As you begin to converse in an intimate manner with God, talking to him about the things that most matter to him and most matter to you (just as you would with a close human friend), you will find yourself naturally moving toward the final step: commitment.

7. *Make a prayer commitment.* Prayer commitment is a decision of the will to convert some aspect of your life. That commitment can be very practical—for example, "Today I will be more patient with my coworkers, especially XX or YY." The best commitments of conversion tend to involve a surrendering of the heart to God, who is calling you to let go of self and embrace him. It may be hard to describe this commitment to yourself or someone else, but when you have made a commitment of conversion, you know it.

I have placed prayer together with sacrifice in this chapter because, as noted above, they are parallel planks of the bridge we lay down so that God can bring us into the fullness of life. They are not tools to create living faith or our other lifestyle remedies, for in the spiritual life we are not *creating* anything—the grace is already there. Instead, they are tools that help us collaborate with Christ's grace in our soul. He is bringing us over the bridge, slowly. He is chipping away at our block of marble with his chisel of grace, and slowly, inauspiciously he draws forth the beautiful, happy man or woman we were created to be. Anyone who has embarked seriously on a life of prayer knows that prayer itself is sacrifice, and through prayer we identify other areas of sacrifice throughout the day that are necessary for our living faith. It's no mystery that sacrifice is an ingredient of every worthwhile endeavor. What you will find gloriously mysterious, however, is how sweet sacrifice can be when done out of love for God, who invites us to leave behind our self-limiting behavior patterns, rest in his Being, and live life to the fullest.

Remember Sarah McGrath from an earlier chapter? Sarah's entrance into living faith was primarily through prayer and sacrifice.

Unlike Jim, who had an identifiable "moment"—a starting point of his baptism in the Spirit—Sarah's first overtures into spirit-filled living came in droplets of unperceived grace in the quiet of her room and while on her knees in church. The spirit-filled people she encountered in the parish opened her up to trying out prayer with a simplicity and sincerity she'd never had before. Previously, prayer had been duty, phrases she repeated in church or around the dinner table—phrases that other people had written. After two years away from her parents and away from church, Sarah certainly wasn't going to pray out of obligation or guilt. When she began to pray again, she now prayed out of a desire to be close to God. There was still guilt about not going to church, but for Sarah—at that stage in her faith—going to church had very little to do with prayer.

Now, guilt can be good or bad. In the form of godly sorrow for our sins (willful offenses against an all-loving God), it is excellent; it is the voice of conscience that keeps us on (or pulls us back to) the straight and narrow road that leads to life in abundance. There's another kind of guilt, however, that's essentially self-pity dipped in fear, and that's the bad form. Sarah's guilty feelings about not going to church had nothing to do with her believing that she was offending God. Instead, her feelings were fruit of an insipid combination of disappointment with herself that she couldn't feel like a good, holy person, and fear that there might be some punishment waiting for her for not doing what her parents and her church told her she must do. Godly sorrow for our sins results in joyful freedom found in forgiveness. The bad kind of guilt leads only to despair.

Under the guidance of her new friends from church and the faith-formation they were receiving, Sarah began to converse with God as with a friend. She learned to have heart-to-heart talks with God about all the things that most mattered to her (from the banalities of daily choices to her deepest desires) and the things she knew mattered most to him. This type of intimate dialogue, outlined in the prayer steps above, is the first mark of true prayer. It is us sons, daughters, and friends of God communicating with our Creator, Father, and Savior in an atmosphere of trust and love. The second mark of prayer is commitment. Intimate dialogue with God uncovers immediately our need to change. We hear God's voice in the silence of our conscience calling out to us to become more like him. In this environment, even his commands are patient invitations. In prayer of dialogue we talk to him about how we can love more. We ask him for strength and courage. We ask forgiveness for our small-minded and selfish behavior.

Prayer marked by intimacy and commitment transforms our outlook and our priorities. This was Sarah's experience. Her first adult encounter with spirit-filled believers and their personal testimony to God's action through prayer encouraged her to start praying. Once she did, she experienced the power of prayer in her own life, not only in answering her needs, but also, and primarily, as a spark of love that grew into a personal relationship with God—a relationship she experienced as being initiated, in a most respectful and patient way, by him. Such intimate dialogue leads naturally to real commitment. In Sarah's case, commitment translated into adjusting her social and professional priorities and rectifying unhealthy relationships. It all happened quite quickly. I was blessed to see her transformation as it developed week by week from spiritual rigidity (caused by fear and guilt) to spontaneous and joyful commitment.

Although her parents' visit reminded her of some of the negative sentiments she was still harboring against them and against her strict upbringing, with time Sarah was able to put aside her resentment. I remember the day she told me she had turned her bitterness over to God. In her words, "I see so clearly now that everything they did for us, they did out of love—even forcing us to go to church without explaining why. How silly of me! I can't believe I was giving them such a hard time when they came to visit. How could they have explained things to us about which they themselves didn't know the answers? They did the best they could, and besides—my gosh!—all things considered, they were excellent parents!"

Had I or anyone else tried to tell Sarah these things just weeks earlier, she never would have been able to accept them. Prayer transforms. God transforms us when we go to him in prayer. A good part of Sarah's living faith occurred through the sacrifice of persevering in prayer, both when she felt spiritual and when she didn't, and then carrying through with the commitments that flowed from her newfound friendship. Her living faith would eventually point her toward deepening her love of God and others through the theological virtues of hope and love.

The ideal I am holding out to you, and to me, of living faith is indeed very high. Perhaps it's even overwhelming, if we haven't yet jumped into the ocean of God's love. When we have finished our overview of all three of our new dispositions of the heart—living faith, living hope, and living love—we will be in a better position to learn simple methods to apply the truths of the Faith-Hope-Love Cure. For now, let it all seep in and trust that God is already beginning a miracle in you.

St. Augustine: Strong Faith from a Healed Intellect

Before moving on to living hope, I want you to read one more story; it is the life of one of my heroes. He was born almost 1,700 years ago, and still his inner journey from shallowness to living faith is strikingly relevant. This spiritual hero is St. Augustine.

The paragraphs below don't do justice to his life story, but I hope they offer enough to encourage you to read his autobiography at a later time. For now, just allow his story to encourage you to continue your own spiritual quest. Times and circumstances change, but God's invitation to put aside shallowness and enter a world of living faith never fails.

St. Augustine of Hippo (AD 354–430) was a lover of all things carnal, and yet he eventually became what we could call the "conqueror of shallowness." He is the ideal hero for the contemporary man or woman who struggles with faith.

Augustine was an unlikely convert, except for the fact that his mom prayed for his conversion for over twenty years! His story reveals a raw, real man whose honest struggles with his human weakness paradoxically testify to human strength, eventually sustained through the grace of God. He is perhaps most well known for his party-loving lifestyle as a young adult, and particularly for his penchant for courting women and enjoying the indulgent pleasures of the flesh (perhaps more typical of his Carthaginian culture than of ours). Like many other men of his day, he had a mistress (whom he seemed to love and respect) and a child by her. Still, he sensed that something about this relationship was off, and he decided to put his extraordinary intellectual gifts to work to uncover the source of discrepancy between the promiscuity and self-indulgent lifestyle that the mainstream culture celebrated and his own desire for authentic happiness.

Augustine was truly a product of his time. He was most pleased by the self-flattering pursuits of academia, at which he excelled. Despite the approval of his culture and the popularity he enjoyed among his friends and intellectual peers, he was unable to shake a nagging desire for spiritual truth. Especially adept at logic and rhetoric, Augustine came to realize that these disciplines in particular were oriented toward winning by one-upping one's opponent, rather than toward discovering the truth. And so he devoted himself to an active quest for truth, attempting to plant the roots of intellectual pursuit in their proper context and diagnosing the popular academic practices of his day as limited in their endlessly circular, self-directed patterns.

In his search for objective truth and for God's call in his life, Augustine turned first toward Manichaeism, a popular theology of his day that saw the world as divided into good (mind) and bad (matter). Though ultimately finding Manichaeism erroneous and converting to Christianity, he realized through his own search that many people, no matter what faith, find truth only after embarking on an arduous quest and that every person, therefore, deserves compassionate assistance in his or her efforts. His early identification with the Manicheans became one of his most important assets as a Christian teacher, allowing him to address and respond wisely and with real understanding to faith-questions throughout the rest of his life. His dealings with the Manicheans offer others a model of profound charity: by example, centuries later, he teaches us to employ patience and understanding as the appropriate methods of engaging people we disagree with, rather than harshness, intolerance, and fanaticism.

An avid lover of beauty, particularly art, philosophy, comedy, literature, and drama, Augustine discovered that an experience of beauty is an experience of the transcendent and of order, and as such it can offer insights into the nature of God. These experiences, combined with the humility bred by his realization of the limitations of human knowledge, confronted Augustine with the smallness of human beings and the grandness of God, who is beyond our comprehension. Paradoxically, he found that this humbling realization was actually liberating and joyful, for what it implied was that if he surrendered everything to God, he could assume his place under God's wing, completely protected and free from the worry of keeping everything under control.

Augustine's real conversion entailed the conquest of his intellectual arrogance, his self-reliance, and his vanity. His example is particularly important for academics, intellectuals, scientists, philosophers, and all who employ reason and logic in their daily quest for truth. Augustine shows us that there is important space for doubt and critical thinking, but that if our intellectual goal is to tear apart everything unverifiable, without allowing for the possibility of philosophical and supernatural truths that we haven't yet grasped, our quest will only consume us and leave us unfulfilled. When Augustine received the gift of faith, not in a miraculous flash of infused spiritual knowledge (as he might have preferred), but rather after honest, laborious inquiry and humble petitioning, he knew he could now grasp reality in a way he never could before. His intellect was not weaker for believing things that carried no physical evidence; on the contrary, it was stronger, for it now could grasp things that a faithless intellect would never understand.

This isn't the place for it, but there is much more that could be said about Augustine's life and how his experience speaks of his deep, living faith. I would encourage you to read his autobiography, *Confessions;* it will inspire you to seek God and the things of God above all else.

Throughout this book, I will point you to spiritual mentors, whether ancient heroes like Augustine, or modern heroes like Jim and Sarah—heroes who overcame their very wounded humanity and now serve as guideposts for us, pointing toward our own potential as spirit-filled people.

I hope that now, before you move forward in this book, you will bow your head or get down on your knees or in some other way give God the sign that you are open to living faith. The difference between life with faith and life without faith is immense. While many nonbelievers struggle to make sense of a life and a world that they believe will end and be no more, the believer approaches the future with limitless hope.

CHAPTER 6

Living Hope

I f you've ever been in or witnessed a relationship where jealousy has taken hold, you know its destructive power.

Mariana and Mark had been dating for over a year when they came to me for help. I knew them pretty well. Both were active members of their respective churches, and although they'd lived in different cities during their whole relationship—Mark in New York and Mariana in Boston—they had grown very close in a relatively short period of time. I'd had the pleasure of being with them as a couple at several social engagements, and I'd been impressed with the way they related to each other. I remember thinking how well matched they were.

Mark was outgoing, determined, ambitious, and very good-natured. A natural leader, he had done exceptionally well in business for his age, not only because of his sharp intellect, great people skills, and zest for calculated risk, but even more because he was a guy you could trust. Just weeks before Mark and Mariana came to see me, the head of Mark' parent company had made him the youngest CEO in the small company's history. Nobody who met Mark for the first time would have known the level of responsibility and stress he carried at work.

Mariana was very smart as well, though quite reserved. In the social situations where I had seen them, she'd usually stayed close to Mark and obviously felt most comfortable listening to and laughing with him or speaking one-on-one with her longtime girlfriends. She took a backseat in group conversations by choice. But any onlooker of those conversations would have picked up quickly on how much Mark respected Mariana's keen intellect and looked to her for affirmation.

Although this time Mark and Mariana came to speak to me together, Mark had come alone once, asking to talk with me after an argument with Mariana had kept him awake all night with nerves. He told me that while he'd been away on business that week, he and Mariana had gotten into an argument via text-messaging that had ended in Mariana making accusations of infidelity and saying, among other things, that she hated him and would never talk to him again. Now, though he'd been home again for some time, she wasn't responding to Mark's texts and calls.

The first thing I asked Jim was why they'd been having such a serious conversation by text-messaging rather than by picking up the phone and working things out—or, better yet, waiting to discuss things in person when he returned. Mark responded that he'd tried to do this but that Mariana typically reverted to texts when she was mad—which, of course, led me to believe that this arguing was not a one-time occurrence. I gave Mark some basic spiritual advice, told him to get some rest, and suggested that he ask Mariana if she'd be willing to come with him next time she was in New York so we could all speak together. Then, after I'd had a chance to hear both sides of the story, we could together determine whether they needed the spiritual guidance I could offer or the aid of a professional relationship counselor.

When Mark and Mariana finally came into my office, I calculated that it had been just over three months since that earlier conversation with Mark. I started out by greeting them both and recalling the good time we'd had together at a concert at the beginning of the year. I then told Mariana that Mark had spoken to me about their earlier argument and asked them both how things had developed since then. Mark stayed quiet and Mariana smiled nervously, looking down as she said, "Not so good."

Mark spoke next, clarifying for me that the argument he'd told me about was no longer an issue: they had worked things out, he said, almost immediately after he and I had spoken at my office. I was surprised that something as serious as accusations of infidelity and the exchange of such harsh words could have blown over in a short time, so I tried to get confirmation from Mariana. "It was worked out for a while," she said, now looking straight at me, "but he keeps doing the same things."

"What things?" I asked. "Are the arguments over the same thing you said Mark had done earlier—being unfaithful?"

She looked at me in confusion, apparently not remembering precisely what I was referring to.

Mark jumped back in. "Father Jonathan, that's exactly the problem. Three months ago the accusation was one thing, and she was sure it had happened; and now she's equally sure it's another thing— another episode of infidelity—even though it turns out the first accusation wasn't true. Every few weeks it's something different. I can't handle it anymore."

I had never seen Mariana be anything but kind and reserved. Now I was about to see another side of her. "I never agreed the other things weren't true," she said harshly. "You're just good at getting out of things and convincing me they never happened, and you know it."

Mark lifted both his palms off his thighs and pointed them upward, his eyes closed in resignation. Clearly this was not the first time they had discussed this. And after a few more probing questions on my part, with communication standoffs at every step, I had no idea how to help. I suggested we call it a day and told them I thought they should see a counselor, because I was pretty convinced this was less a spiritual problem and more one of communication.

Mariana got one last dig in at Mark before they left, saying that no counselor could help them unless Mark started being honest with himself and her. Mark, the indomitable and even-tempered business whiz, was reduced to a pitiful ball of quiet tears.

Two days later, out of the corner of my eye I saw Mark and Mariana together having a great time laughing and holding hands at a neighborhood establishment near my home. I discreetly kept my distance—too soon, too awkward.

But then for a few weeks I didn't see Mark at church. Eventually I got a call from Mariana. She wanted to drive down to New York from Boston to talk. I could tell she was suffering and I, of course, assumed that it was about a problem with Mark. But her suffering voice was not frantic and angry as it had been weeks before in my office. It was intensely sad.

FINDING HOPE IN A DISTRUSTFUL WORLD

I'll get back to Mariana and Mark's story in a moment, but first I would like to situate it in the context of this chapter. We have seen how *living faith* can heal our intellect of shallowness and form within us the habit of seeing and judging things as God does. Now we will consider how the theological virtue of hope can heal our memories and help us establish a lifestyle of *living hope,* where fear-based and shame-based thought and behavior patterns no longer rule our lives.

I don't think I need to convince you that distrust is a growing epidemic in our society and is partly to blame for the crumbling of the institutions of marriage and family in the Western world. If you can't trust, you don't commit. And if you don't commit, you yourself are less worthy of trust. So goes the vicious cycle.

Instead of continuing the cycle, we need to ask what is at the heart of our trust issues and what we can do about the problem. Can we blame trust issues on our frantic world? Today's global security threats, the financial instability plaguing businesses large and small, and the personal failures of government and church leaders give us lots of excuses to distrust others and retreat in fear to protect ourselves at all cost. But how do these contemporary sources of fear compare to those of ages past? Can we say with any certainty that we have more reasons to fear for our well-being now than fifty, one hundred, or two hundred years ago? Surely new trends in communication technology bring to our attention more evil than in previous generations (the twenty-four-hour news cycle, anonymous vitriol in Internet forums and chat rooms, a Babylon of conflicting opinions, etc.), but today's society also provides us greater health technology, financial potential, and independence than in any other period in history. Relatively speaking, today we have very few reasons to be afraid. And yet we are terrified on so many levels.

We are terrified, I believe, not so much because of any external threats, but rather because we don't trust each other; we don't trust ourselves or our neighbors to be there for each other in hard times.

Our vivid memories of past betrayals and personal failures constantly tell us that self-protection and maintaining our status quo is less painful than exposing ourselves to further betrayal and failure. Just as a deer is mesmerized by light even as it stands in harm's way, so a fearful, distrusting person stands frozen by potential threats he creates as real and present in his own mind, because he remembers the past. As I will explain in this chapter, the sister of "fear" and "anxiety" is "shame" and I will treat them as a package, the former two being most prevalent in women (though not exclusively) and the latter in men (again, not exclusively), and all being healed by God's grace through living hope.

I propose living hope as the second disposition of the heart. It flows out of living faith, but not automatically; we have to work at it. Living hope is about breaking free from our self-imposed limits through trust in God's promises to us. Self-help readers will at first find this similar to the New Age principles of "the Law of Attraction" and "the Secret"—principles by which, according to their proponents, we reach out into the universe, decide what we want from it, and then let it go so that it might come back to us. Over the last few years, millions of copies of self-help books based on these principles have been sold in America and around the world. According to these books, people who live "the Secret" are able to transcend perceived limitations and get whatever they want out of life. When you have attained the secret of living your desired destiny, you will automatically overcome all obstacles to what you can acquire or become.

Living hope is so similar, but yet so different! It is the habit of living with the certain and life-giving knowledge that God has great things in store for us and is on our side, encouraging us to claim those benefits as our own. Living hope is moving forward toward attaining things we think are good for us, while simultaneously abandoning our desires to God's will, free from the fear that God and his plans are not enough to make us fully happy, whatever they are. This is not the same as being an optimist. Optimism and pessimism are mere emotional states of the soul, as we saw earlier; they come and go for many different reasons that we can't always control. Living hope, on the other hand, involves using intelligence and free will to press forward fearlessly and shamelessly toward our goals, with absolute peace and confidence in God's care for us no matter what happens!

Seared into the human psychology is the desire for security and for success. The temptation of our fallen nature is to procure these on our own terms. Here lies the secret of Christian hope—we are confident *first* in God and only then in ourselves as his Junior Partners, for whom he has marvelous plans. This is real self-confidence: knowing that God is on our side.

In the living of this new disposition of the heart, we confront an existential irony in the apparent conflict between our natural mechanisms of memory and imagination, on the one hand—mechanisms that remind us of human limitations and past failings—and the call to trust in God's promises, on the other. For it is precisely in exposing and submitting ourselves to the unknown and invisible, under the care and mercy of God, that we find true security. It is in risking safety and self-image by letting go of every dream and every pleasure outside of God's plans that we find true success.

In every possible way, Jesus invites us to live audaciously outside of our comfort zone—to reach out to the universe, so to speak, and claim it, not as our own, but rather as a gift to be enjoyed by Junior Partners of the Holy Spirit in the work of salvation history. Living hope moves us to live fully our role as temporal custodians of God's creation and co-agents in our own earthly and eternal destiny. What an exciting adventure! God has chosen you and me to be his hands and feet, to go about the world doing good and to have a wonderful time of it.

But living hope should not be confused with risk-taking. Gamblers are successful if they can regularly beat the odds, if they can limit the risk and maximize opportunity. Christians who audaciously seek out and then place themselves in the center of God's plan are not gamblers, because we aren't betting against odds—they're all on our side. We know the ultimate outcome before the dice are thrown, and that outcome is in our favor.

Yet *still* we freeze! This new disposition of the heart—living hope—thaws us out, makes us nimble, prepares us for heroic action, and allows us to smile even as we suffer, knowing that God is on the side both of the righteous and of the humble sinner, and he will act in his perfect timing and according to his perfect knowledge of what we need.

One of the great enemies of living hope is what St. Paul calls "prudence of the flesh" (Romans 6:8, NASB). Another word for this is "sophistry"—that is, deceptive reasoning. False prudence usually comes in the form of groundless but genuine-sounding excuses that give us an out and lead us back to fear-based and shame-based self-protection. Prudence of the flesh always gives us more-or-less convincing reasons why we shouldn't commit ourselves fully to what we have good reason to believe is God's will for us.

Let's apply the goal of living hope to Mariana's story. Mariana's humble disposition as she entered my office on her own for the first time was a stark contrast to the aggression and anger I had witnessed from her when she and Mark came to visit me together. Although she was obviously sad, at a deeper level this Mariana was more like the happy Mariana I had seen in public, so deeply in love with her boyfriend. Her brokenness begged for empathy, and her profound goodness as a person was on full display. I had no idea what crisis had occurred to bring her to this point, but deep down I knew something *good* had also happened, for genuine brokenness always bodes well for growth.

"Mark broke up with me," she said, her shoulders slumping as she sighed.

After the breakup, she explained, she had done some serious soul-searching. She relived in her mind the many great moments they had shared together, and—most painful—also the fights. She pored over, then deleted, the angry, accusatory text messages she had sent in the various arguments they'd had in recent months.

"I feel so terrible," she said. "He didn't deserve this, and I screwed everything up."

"How did things end?" I asked her, searching for some angle from which I could at least console.

"We got in another stupid fight, and he told me he couldn't handle it anymore. He said I needed to get help if we're ever going to have a real relationship, but he seemed convinced that's not possible."

As Mariana and I continued to discuss her rocky relationship with Mark, it became clear to me that while usually it takes two to tango, Mark had done the right thing in breaking things off with Mariana. She confessed to me that the accusations she had made about Mark's infidelity weren't based on what most people would consider evidence. Despite that, in her mind, in the moment, she had all the proof she needed.

"If you don't mind," I asked, "what kind of evidence did you have?"

Mariana couldn't remember exactly, she said, but it had to do with him not spending as much time with her as she would have liked, especially on important occasions, other "fishy" things he would do, and also the way his female coworkers corresponded with him in a sometimes frivolous, personal manner.

Sensing that Mariana still needed to pinpoint the heart of the problem, I asked her to describe to me when, or under what circumstances, her doubts about Mark had typically surfaced. After some thinking, she said she never doubted him when she was with him; the doubts came when she was missing him and when he didn't express to her how much he loved and missed her. The fights were usually triggered by a text message that she would throw out to, as she said, test him. When he didn't answer appropriately, Mariana considered his weak response to be a confirmation of all the worst-case scenarios she had played out in her head. Furthermore, his response in the moment would link up instantaneously, in Mariana's mind, with all the earlier times he had acted similarly; and this juxtaposition would fortify her subjective conclusions. It wasn't just about now for Mariana; it was the overall picture—no, *feeling*—of betrayal that would kick her emotions into high gear and trigger an onslaught of what Mark experienced as a crazy and irrational outburst.

Because Mark knew that all this vitriol was uncharacteristic of Mariana, he put up with it for quite a while. As soon as they met again in person, Mariana would be herself again, and apologize profusely for her behavior. (This explained to me why I had seen Mark and Mariana so happy together just two days after what I had considered a terribly unproductive meeting in my office.)

I told Mariana I thought she was now in a very good position, a much better position than if she were still together with Mark. She gave me a disbelieving roll of the eyes, let out a small sigh, and sat way back in the chair as if trying to disappear. I then told Mariana what she already knew at some level—that the real Mariana was the kind, loving, smart, adoring, stabilizing woman I knew and with whom Mark had fallen in love. Every few weeks, the unhappy convergence of distance from Mark, inconsiderate and sometimes selfish action by Mark, and the speed and detached nature of text-messaging would trigger behavior that was completely out of line with her character. When she acted in this way, she was out of herself; her emotions were manipulating her free will.

The good news, I told her—besides the fact that this wasn't the real Mariana—was that she was only partially responsible for this destructive behavior and thus shouldn't beat herself up over it. When our free will is manipulated by uncontrollable forces, our moral responsibility diminishes. This is probably why Mark was so forgiving of Mariana after her outbursts. He was confident that Mariana wasn't really like this when she was able to reason. But I also explained to Mariana that diminished moral responsibility in such cases doesn't free us from full social and interpersonal responsibility, and certainly not from the consequences of our actions, as Mariana found out when Mark said he'd had enough. Moreover, even if moral responsibility is diminished in moments of blind passion, *overall* moral responsibility of a person given to such behavior actually increases as that person realizes what he or she is capable of in the future if things aren't brought under control now.

The long and short of my work with Mariana was for her to find the root cause of her self-defeating behavior. As we found out together over the next weeks, the cause was *fear* of betrayal, manifested (mostly in her mind) as uncontrollable jealousy.

Although I didn't tell Mariana, I was confident she and Mark would someday be back together. It would depend on her willingness to open herself up to God's help, a willingness that would determine not only the outcome of this relationship, but also the degree of her personal freedom and happiness, culminating in living hope, where she could live free from fear and realize her outstanding potential.

Oprah Winfrey made famous a man named Eckhart Tolle by featuring his books on her show in 2008 and choosing him among her spiritual gurus. He is the author of several bestsellers in the self-help genre. While respecting his ability to communicate deep things in simple terms, I find reading him quite painful, because he effectively draws in people with helpful and true intuitions about the human soul and self-improvement, and then, in my estimation, steers people back to themselves and away from the ultimate source of transformation and redemption that can be found in an all-loving and all-powerful God. Self-help divorced from God-help—whether Tolle's approach or another—always comes up short.

Some of Tolle's techniques for self-analysis and behavioral change are worth highlighting here, especially with Mariana's story still fresh in our minds. Tolle teaches how to stop yourself when you get emotionally upset so that what he calls your "pain-body" doesn't drive your actions. He suggests that you pause and observe yourself. This, he says, is a way of tapping into the real you—the you who observes yourself. Stepping back from negative emotions like anger, envy, and fear can help you become centered again and to remember that you're part of a bigger plan (though he isn't specific as to what bigger plan that is).

Tolle wisely places a lot of emphasis on not being offended by the actions of others. He says that when people display a condescending, disapproving, or malicious attitude toward you, it's their ego or "pain-body" driving them. By recognizing where their actions are coming from, you can rise above the situation and realize that you don't have to let those actions affect you. It's a way of emotionally removing yourself from the offense so that it doesn't bother you. He points out that this is similar to Jesus's teaching to "turn the other cheek" (Matt. 5:39).

These suggestions are valid and helpful, properly understood. Experience and faith tell us, however, that this mind-over-matter approach won't be long-lasting in most people. This is true because most of our "pain-body" behavior, as in Mariana's case, won't change substantially by simply *willing* it to. Over the long haul, unless we uncover the rotting roots of our interior life that make us some combination of shallow, fearful, shameful, and/or self-centered, we won't experience a truly flourishing life.

If, on the other hand, we invite God to heal us—usually through a long process of conversion (a series of decisions of the will to reverse course, as in the process of making straight the path) followed by the miracle of God's grace in what we have called the Faith-Hope-Love Cure—there is a real chance for radical transformation. Eckhart Tolle and Oprah Winfrey get it right that "pain-body" behavior is not the best "us," but their solutions will always be weak as long as they point us back only to ourselves, instead of to ourselves *in union with our Creator*.

Let's continue to use Mariana's story to see how, in her case, this conversion and cure I speak of might take place. Keep in mind, Mariana was already a woman of strong faith, even living faith, when she became involved with Mark. God was a very real part of her life. Despite that, she was stuck, frozen with fear. Her condition affected her faith such that she sometimes doubted whether her past and present experiences of God were genuine. The interconnectivity of the theological virtues makes discerning where we are and what we need tricky. Mariana was tempted to deny God's power in her life because her faith in him wasn't translating into the deep happiness she so desired. This doesn't mean, however, that she wasn't a woman of living faith. She was a woman of faith *who needed hope!*

Make Straight the Path: Mariana's Version

Now let's take another pass through Mariana's story and see how she's navigating the six steps of the earlier-described Make Straight the Path process. As we look at each of the stages in turn, her problems—and her attempts to reach a faith-filled solution—may offer us some help in our own struggles.

1. *Make a searching and fearless moral inventory of your life.* In coming to speak to me, Mariana had already begun the process of making an honest inventory of her life. It wasn't quite searching and fearless yet, but sometimes the first step is the hardest! She now needs to move away from seeing self-improvement only in relation to Mark and the apparent failure of their relationship. Her inventory should include other relationships in her life, past and present (and not just romantic ones), focusing on those in which trust has been broken or fear of betrayal has gripped her. Because we are very poor judges of ourselves and therefore tend to formulate revisionist, untrue histories of our past, a searching and fearless inventory is most complete when we ask people close to us for their version of our stories.

2. *Admit to God, to yourself, and to other human beings the exact nature of your wrongs and your powerlessness over them.*

Mariana's admission to God, herself, and other human beings needn't be a drama-filled opening of old wounds. Whereas a longtime drinker or addict usually leaves a trail of suffering in his wake and has a responsibility to make serious reparation, those of us confronting a relatively minor life crisis, as Mariana is doing, can direct our admissions primarily to God and ourselves. If a natural and comfortable opportunity comes along for Mariana to apologize to other people for the ways her fear, insecurities, and jealousy have affected them, this may be a good thing to pursue. But it isn't usually necessary and sometimes can do more damage than good. The second part of this step for Mariana would be to recognize her powerlessness over the fear. An outside observer would easily see that her loss of Mark, whom she deeply loved, on account of her paranoia is proof of her powerlessness. But in the field of personal conversion, outside observers don't count. Mariana needs to come to accept this on her own. Powerlessness here doesn't mean uselessness; it simply means we need help.

3. *Turn your will over to God's care and live trusting that he can make you whole.* Mariana is a woman of faith and therefore would seem to have little work to do in being open to the fact that God can make her whole. But here again, there are different degrees of openness and belief in God's power, and great faith in God doesn't always translate into faith that he can transform *me*! When we find ourselves in moments of crisis of any kind, we have a choice to either retreat away from God into our world of

self-pity or retreat away from our broken world into the hands of God. If Mariana increases her prayer time now, she surely will increase also her belief in God's power to make her whole.

4. *Begin to live the New Commandment: "Love one another as I have loved you."* As a practicing Christian, Mariana has surely made at least an unconscious decision to turn her will and life over to God's care and to live the New Commandment. But this step of the Make Straight the Path process cannot be unconscious or assumed. Even if Mariana has at many points in the past invited God into her life, she may never have invited him to have his way with her in her areas of weakness, now much more evident than in the past. Personal crisis opens us up to new levels of positive surrender. It's easy to say that we believe in God when we have a firm grip on the reins of our lives and when the future looks bright. It's not so easy to say, "God, I give the reins over to you, no matter where you may lead me," when the path is strewn with boulders and night is falling.

5. *Make amends to anyone you have harmed along the way with your selfish pursuits.* Mariana has probably hurt herself more than anyone else, but even so, it's important that she ask herself if she's willing to make amends to anyone she has harmed along the way. "Willingness" is the operative word here. Even as unattractive as our faults can be—fear and jealousy, in Mariana's case—we attach ourselves to them. We find it hard to live without them and *very* hard to make amends for the damage they have caused. This step is a sur-

rendering of our old way of being. "I no longer want to be the possessive girlfriend. I give it up," Mariana needs to say. "I let it go. I make amends, or at least I am willing to make amends, for having been what I used to be."

6. *Design and follow a practical plan to hold yourself accountable to God and to others.* This last of our self-help steps of conversion will be the hardest for Mariana. She is smart—very smart—and is used to taking care of herself; furthermore, she is private and reserved. Once she has worked through the first five steps, Mariana will need to make a heroic effort to involve other people in her plan for self-improvement. She will need to bare her soul to people she trusts about her own weaknesses and pitfalls. In future relationships, and especially if she ends up back with Mark, she will need to set parameters, known to others, that will help her avoid obsessive, fear-based patterns.

Despite the many times I have mentioned this already, I don't think I can overstate that these six steps of conversion, of path-straightening, will not make Mariana, or anyone else, a spirit-filled person. They will not bring her to life in abundance. But they *will* allow her to face the problem at hand and prepare her for a miracle of grace through the theological virtue of hope. The miracle she needs, one that usually comes with time and hard work, is freedom from fear through a healing of her memory. That will allow her to trust in God's promises that he is enough for her, regardless of how others have behaved toward her in the past.

Mariana's experience of anxiety and fear was relational in nature, but these emotions can be just as paralyzing in other fields of our lives—for example, in connection with health issues, job security, or public speaking. Living hope heals our memory such that knowledge of the past no longer disproportionately dictates how we decide to deal with the present. The woman of living faith remembers her past failings but does not freeze in front of today's challenges. She has no reason to fear because she no longer depends on chance or her own ability alone to make things right. She relies on God's being faithful to his promises to be with her and to bring her to her fulfillment.

FEAR'S VARIED MANIFESTATIONS

In women, fear is most often manifested in anxiety, distrust, panic, jealousy, and low self-image. In men, it is most often manifested in shame or shame-based behavior (the avoidance of shame at all cost). This is not to say men don't get anxious or jealous or that women are never ashamed. Still, the two big patterns in the sexes are undeniable.

And this gender difference has consequences, especially when it's not understood by the parties to a relationship. Countless books have been written about the importance of communication in relationships. I can't tell you how many women tell me their husbands don't know how to communicate; likewise, men often tell me they prefer *not* to communicate as their wives would like them to, because all of the "serious talks" they finally agree to end up causing more problems! While *good* communication is important for all relationships, "good" does not equal "lots of." The most important thing for a healthy relationship is learning to understand—intellectually and emotionally—how one's spouse or significant other *experiences* the issue at hand.

Mark saw Mariana's outbursts as "irrational," and at one level they were. But "irrational" doesn't mean "stupid" or "unreal." Mariana was reacting to *something* (we can't *react* to *nothing*), and yet as long as Mark considered her reaction to be in direct relation to what she accused him (falsely) of doing, he would always be confused. Mariana was reacting out of fear of what could be, but wasn't yet. Mariana's accusations were unfounded in this case, but she had good reason to wonder if indeed her fears were grounded in truth because her memory was constantly reminding her of what had happened in the past—not only in other relationships (perceived rejection), but also at the beginning of theirs (dishonesty on Mark's part, revealed to me only late in our conversations together).

Once in a while we hear a shocking story in the news of a father who abandons his large family, leaving no explanation. One morning the wife and mother wakes up and he's gone. Apparently, no warning signs were seen. He's just not there.

Have you noticed that these sad stories generally come at the worst possible moment for the family? The wife has lost her job, a child is sick, bills are due, a baby is on the way, etc. Compound tragedies! Our first reaction is to think what a jerk the guy must be. How could anyone leave his wife and kids in such a moment! This is precisely when the kids need him; it's when the couple needs to stick together. Adding insult to injury, these stories usually end with the husband found bellied up to the bar or at the casino, or maybe watching football with college buddies. These guys on the lam may or may not be jerks, but their sudden retreat from the battlefield doesn't *prove* that they are. Men cannot stand shame. The thought of watching a wife and family suffer because of his own ineptness is every decent man's worst nightmare, and sometimes the pain of it is overwhelming.

The "masculine" version of fear and anxiety presents itself as this sort of shame. Tell this to a man, though, and he will probably recoil at the thought. *Shame? What's that?* As much as we men hate to admit that the avoidance of shame is a major factor in our behavior and mental patterns, it is dominant in our lives. Shame-based behavior is rooted in the fear of failure. Nobody likes to fail, of course, but failure affects men in a very special way, threatening a self-image of successful provider and protector that we naturally and desperately want to preserve. Compare the two columns below. The first represents a negative outcome that nobody would want. The second represents a subjective experience of shame—no, *fear* of shame—that is much more painful than the failure itself would be. It is this fear of shame that causes men to flee failure at almost any cost, or to make up for failure by doing something, *anything,* that will make the feelings go away.

Unemployment	"I got fired."
Being alone / single	"Nobody wants me." / "She dumped me."
Broken marriage / family	"I blew it: I couldn't protect my family."
Sickness, pain	"I now depend on others."
Bad grades / poor education	"People think I'm stupid."
Unattractive physique	"Nobody could love me like this."
Debt	"I'm a loser; I've lost control."

The biblical character Job is one of the best known in all of scripture. He is often referred to in sermons and literature as the prototype of patience. While I have my doubts about how naturally patient he was, he was first and foremost a man of living hope. He waited upon the Lord because he trusted that God would be faithful to his promises!

You'll remember that Job is the innocent one whom God tested with every kind of suffering imaginable. The devil was convinced Job worshipped God only because things were going well for him, and made a bet with God that he could make Job deny his faith if God would allow him, the devil, to bring calamity upon Job. God took up the offer, probably to teach the rest of us a lesson. Job remained faithful—he didn't curse God—but boy did he suffer.

> I loathe my life;
> I will give free utterance to my complaint;
> I will speak in the bitterness of my soul.
> I will say to God, Do not condemn me;
> let me know why you contend against me.
> Does it seem good to you to oppress,
> to despise the work of your hands
> and favor the schemes of the wicked?
> Why did you bring me forth from the womb?
> Would that I had died before any eye had seen me,
> and were as though I had not been,
> carried from the womb to the grave.
> Are not the days of my life few?
> Let me alone, that I may find a little comfort
> before I go, never to return,
> to the land of gloom and deep darkness,
> where light is like darkness. (Job 10:1–3, 18–22, NRSV)

When *we* say the things Job said, it's usually because we're depressed. But that wasn't Job's case! Just the opposite—he was full of hope in the midst of objective tragedy and horrifically ugly feelings.

Job had *every* good reason to want to die. He lost all of his riches overnight, his children died of natural disasters, many of his friends abandoned him, and he himself became deathly sick (see Job 1:13–2:13). Then add to all of this the fact that the devil was dedicated to telling him lies about the God in whom he believed, and you'll get a taste of how miserable Job was.

So why didn't Job curse God, as his wife suggested: "Curse God, and die" (Job 2:9)? Because he knew God's promises and he trusted their source—God himself! When he made his list of good things in life, he included *supernatural truths*. His faith was so strong that he believed in God's *unfailing* love for him. Job knew God in a personal way, and because he did, he trusted that his all-loving, all-powerful Friend must have a bigger, better plan, even if Job himself couldn't yet see it or even imagine what it could be.

Most men don't react as Job did to calamity, unfortunately. I know a gentleman in his late forties with more postgraduate degrees to his name than the University of Michigan football team has national championships (eleven). Go Blue! Well, he doesn't actually have that many degrees, but the number isn't far off. Gregory kept going back to school, much to the chagrin of his fiancée, saying that he hadn't yet found his niche. After years of this, Gregory's fiancée finally forced him to make a decision about whether they would get married, and they did. The discontent didn't go away, though, and now Gregory could no longer skirt the issue of why he never was satisfied in the workplace. He had worked as an engineer, an architect, and a lawyer and, although he never admitted it, he disliked all three professions because he felt he wasn't good at any of them. He knew he excelled in school, and that's where he always longed to be.

It's a painful but very helpful exercise for men (and women) to review why we don't do what we know we should do. Think for a moment about the things your wife, boss, or church has been asking you repeatedly to do. Once we get over our knee-jerk reaction to excuse our behavior on account of a lack of time or resources, we will find on many occasions that we're procrastinating because we don't know how to do something or are afraid to fail.

ON THE ROAD TO HEALING

When we begin to let living hope have its way with us, focusing more on all the *good* God wants to do for us and with us, and less on past failures or on our own limited abilities to change the present, our fears slowly begin to subside. It takes time to get used to getting our minds out of God's way like this. Repeated acts of faith and hope in God's love, power, and desire to bring us happiness have the effect of enlarging our comfort zone. Newly free from the immediate and overwhelming power of shame and anxiety, but still partially in its clutches, we no longer are preoccupied with protecting self-image above all else. Instead, we concern ourselves with imaging God in self, forging our character to mirror him, out of love for him who has begun to make us whole again.

The gradual subsiding of fear and the expansion of our comfort zone happen contemporaneously. If we wait for one to drive the other, we will never experience change. Beginning to hope now, even if our hope is simple, prepares us for the disposition of living hope that will sustain us no matter what comes our way. Men and women of living hope see good and bad fortune as divine lifelines lifting us out of the ordinary and preparing us for something much bigger and better. The unexpected storms—even when we learn to see them, paradoxically, as lifelines—are scary, for sure; but when we trust God in all things, life is very good, because our future, if not our present, is full of light.

Have you ever noticed that people in some of the poorest countries seem to react best to tragedy? Whether the catastrophe be in Haiti, Indonesia, or sub-Saharan Africa, news reporters covering natural or human-caused disasters in undeveloped or developing countries regularly communicate, with great surprise, how "resilient" the residents are. These reporters usually parachute into ground zero for a few days and try their best to put themselves in the shoes of the locals in order to tell their story. Although news stations are often criticized for it, "parachuting in" is not always a bad thing. The cultural contrast of foreign reporters with their surroundings often allows them to tell a part of the story a local reporter might not find newsworthy, such as the amazing resiliency of the people. No matter how seasoned the reporters are, we almost always hear them express their disbelief at how the locals bounce back so quickly and so well, helping themselves and one another and learning to smile again.

From what I have seen in covering stories of this nature, as well as in witnessing smaller-scale personal and family tragedies, this "resiliency" is not directly related to the material poverty of the people. Poverty itself doesn't make anyone resilient or good. The ability to bounce back has more to do with the "spiritual humility" of the individual who is living the disaster, a quality and virtue we easily lose in an affluent, materialistic society. Spiritual humility is the virtue of healthy, emotional detachment from personal image and things—even good things like health, fine food, reputation, and nice shelter. That sort of humility grants freedom from the clutches of extraneous things, such that we spontaneously distinguish between the essential and the contingent and thus can live with or without unnecessary things.

In poorer countries residents, both the rich and the poor, are in contact with people who have very little. If their eyes and hearts are open, they usually are aware of someone right around the corner who is worse off than they are. They also see the curious fact that some poor and sick people are sad and angry, while others are happy and free. When tragedy hits a person who has reflected on these things and has learned to be detached from possessing unnecessary things (even good things), he more quickly stands up, dusts himself off, and sets his sights on building a better life. He hasn't lost hope, because he knows that as long as he has life, he still has capacity for the two great, necessary human "events": loving and being loved. When tragedy hits someone who considers herself entitled to getting everything she wants, or someone unable to distinguish between the essential and the contingent, resentment and anger make getting up and starting over almost impossible, until the mirage of self-sufficiency dissolves.

Although resiliency, as described above, is a mere human virtue, it is supported and enhanced by the theological virtues, and indeed is a big part of living hope. To this point, it isn't happenstance that suffering societies and individuals tend to be more religious than their more "successful" counterparts. The cynical explanation would be that God is the "crutch" of the poor and oppressed, as if crutches were bad and for the weak of mind. Meanwhile, those who think they are young, beautiful, rich, and healthy just forget about (or make numb) their weakness and need for help. Success is the preferred drug of the proud. When everything is going our way, we fall into the stupor of self-sufficiency. But self-sufficiency is false hope. It is building a house on a bad foundation. It is betting on the immortality of mortals. Self-sufficiency is the precursor of desperation.

When we are spiritually grounded, on the other hand, we feel sufficient in God. We are unafraid of our own weakness. We "rejoice in our sufferings," as St. Paul said (Rom. 5:3, RSV). We lean on Jesus as a friend who is happy to be our crutch in tough times.

The journey of living hope requires of us little, ongoing decisions to trust in God. It requires the courage to get in the game of hope even when we aren't yet very good at it. Starting into living hope is a bit like volleying with a great tennis coach. We serve him our best shot, as weak as it may be, and he returns it with a little more power and always just within our reach. We scramble to get into position and send the ball back as best we can. He calculates our point of weakness and drops the shot perfectly to test that same weakness. In time we see some progress: the more we play, the better we get. Diving into living hope is our way of telling the divine Coach that we want him to raise us to his level. We tell him to show us what we're capable of and how good life can be as his Junior Partner.

In the final chapter, we will look at ways that we can make living hope—along with living faith and living love—a part of our daily routine. With the application of those theological virtues, we will learn to confront our most common sources of fear and shame and bring them to the great Healer, who can't wait for us to become happy and whole.

First, however, we will confront *living love* as the completion and climax of the Faith-Hope-Love Cure. St. Paul's teaching on the primacy of love could not be stronger: "If I speak with the tongues of men and of angels, but do not have love, I have become a noisy gong or a clanging cymbal" (1 Cor. 13:1, NASB).

CHAPTER 7

Living Love

Followers of Madame Blavatsky, a nineteenth-century woman whom many consider the mother of New Age spirituality, say her teachings can be boiled down to one word: compassion. Compassion as the highest destination of the human heart runs through the best of contemporary New Age and self-help books. There's something very right about this intuition. After all, have you ever met a man or woman of deep compassion who wasn't genuinely good in many other ways? Compassion is always found next to tolerance, understanding, and mercy. Imagine a world full of people who were like that all the time! The compassionate soul's ability to "suffer with"—as the Latin roots *com* ("with") and *passio* ("suffering") imply—is a fertilizer for a beautiful garden of virtues.

The problem with reducing our spiritual progress to acquiring compassion is that compassion is predominantly a *feeling,* an emotional state of our soul that can come and go without our say. As a sentiment, it finds itself outside the parameters of our will and therefore at some level outside of our reach. If Jesus asks "perfection" of us Christians—remember our discussion of "Be perfect, therefore, as your heavenly Father is perfect" in chapter 4—and if we are unable at times to attain compassion no matter what we say or do, we can be confident that the ideal he asks of us can be found someplace other than in compassion.

But Madame Blavatsky and her many followers were not far off. Compassion is a wonderful and common fruit of holy souls who have learned to love with the heart of God.

Deepak Chopra is another famed author of New Age spirituality who sees compassion or "goodness" toward others as a key to happiness. His book *The Seven Spiritual Laws of Success* has been a bestseller for many years. Chopra has a talent for packaging age-old principles in attractive, practical language. One of his seven laws is "the Law of Giving." He explains the value of giving to others in this way:

> The Law of Giving and Receiving is simple: If you want love, learn to give love; if you want attention and appreciation, learn to give attention and appreciation; if you want material affluence, help others to become materially affluent. If you want to be blessed with all the good things in life, learn to silently bless everyone with all the good things in life. The more you give, the more you will receive. (p. 31–32)

Chopra's Law of Giving definitely moves us beyond the field of sentiments or feelings. His law sounds quite similar, in fact, to the Golden Rule: "Do unto others as you would have them do unto you." What a great law this is! Anyone who lives it is well on her way to natural happiness, and is well prepared for spirit-filled living, or beatitude.

But as right and good as Blavatsky's and Chopra's teachings are in reference to interpersonal relations, they are light-years away from the Christian disposition of *living love,* the subject of this chapter.

The highest call of the human soul is a continuous decision of the will to love others and to allow ourselves to be loved by them, no matter the positive or negative sentiments we may feel (Blavatsky), and not because of the good consequences this will bring upon ourselves (Chopra). Love (sometimes called "charity") is the theological virtue that heals our selfish will. As we saw in the preceding two chapters, faith heals our intellect and hope heals our memory.

FOLLOWING JESUS'S MODEL OF REDEMPTIVE LOVE

The sacrificial life and death of Jesus Christ is the ultimate contrast to contemporary, feelings-based or consequences-based conceptions of love. Self-help books evoke Jesus's message of love, but very few dare to flesh out what this message is.

For Jesus, love is self-giving to the other, for the sake of the other!

- "I came not to be served but to serve." (Matt. 20:28, NRSV)

- "Whoever does not take up their cross and follow me is not worthy of me." (Matt. 10:38, NIV)

- "Amen, amen, I say to you, unless a grain of wheat falls to the ground and dies, it remains just a grain of wheat; but if it dies, it produces much fruit." (John 12:24, NAB)

Living love, in the mode of Jesus of Nazareth, is our third new disposition of the heart. As stated above, it is the lifestyle remedy for selfishness. Love invites us to reevaluate our relationships in reference to our vocation as *lovers* in the way of Jesus: with a love that is *personal, selfless,* and *redemptive.*

Jesus's way of love was personal. He came to redeem all humanity, but chose to work with one sinner at a time. With a whole world to save, he found time to rub mud on the eyes of the blind, dine with a lonely tax collector, train a motley group of twelve, turn water into wine, defend the guilty, make friends with women and men—and weep too. The new, self-giving disposition of the heart is a call to love others, not only because God dwells within them, but because of *who they are,* beloved by God and of his design. Living love, as a disposition of the heart, allows us to see people as God sees them, love them as God loves them, one neighbor, coworker, boss, spouse, and child at a time.

Even after many years of marriage—even very good marriage—living love with your spouse is a huge challenge. Ana, a woman from Upper Michigan who has been married for more than forty years, recently told me how the last two years of her relationship with her husband had been more difficult than the previous forty-two combined. Ana's husband, Lionel, had worked as an engineer in the auto industry— with one company, for that matter—his entire career. Although I didn't know Lionel well, when Ana was describing their difficulties I could picture him from the times he'd attended events where I was speaking. What I most remembered were all the writing instruments, of various sizes, colors, and purposes, he carried in his front shirt pocket in an oversize plastic pocket protector. He's the only person I've ever met who carried on him at all times both a geometry compass and a land compass!

Lionel was the consummate engineer. He was ultra-careful to speak with perfect grammar and admirable precision of vocabulary. The phonetic result was as many pauses between words as words in his sentence. It was quite refreshing, actually, because you knew everything he was saying had a good purpose. If I hadn't been told otherwise, I would have thought he hated to listen to me speak, because after each talk I was always in for a thorough critique of my presentation. But he did it in such a good-spirited and accurate way that I found it endearing.

Ana loved Lionel greatly. She loved his intelligence and his heart of gold. She even came to appreciate his quirks. But two years ago, Ana explained, Lionel had been let go from General Motors. It was a shock to everyone. Ana was resentful when she heard the news, because he had given his life to this company and they were letting him go two years before his planned retirement. A few weeks after the news was handed down, however, one of Lionel's colleagues went to visit Ana and confirmed her greatest fear. Lionel had been let go not because of the economic woes of the company, as had been explained to Lionel, but rather because they could no longer depend on him to remember basic things about his work. The visitor explained to Ana that for the last six months Lionel's coworkers had been covering for him as he began to repeat himself and become increasingly forgetful in front of clients and the bosses. Ana had noticed some of this at home, but since Lionel followed such a rigorous routine, he managed quite well—so well that Ana had been concerned that *she* was the one being forgetful.

Ana eventually took Lionel to see a specialist, who confirmed that Lionel was experiencing the first stages of dementia, almost certainly Alzheimer's disease. The dementia progressed much more rapidly than the doctors had predicted. Now, two years into his retirement, Ana was at her wits' end. Most people had no idea Lionel was even sick, so hers was a solitary suffering. Like many Alzheimer's patients, Lionel was good at keeping things straight and coming across quite well in social

settings. He steered clear of "confusing" topics and personal relationships and instead focused on canned phrases and reactions that gave
him security.

By the time Ana came to me she was steaming with anger toward
Lionel. He was driving her nuts. "It's up to thirty times a day now," she
said passionately, with a look that revealed a combination of anger and
guilt. "He's constantly asking me, 'What are we supposed to do now?'
I feel like telling him, 'Crazy people don't have anything to do, so stop
asking.'" I was surprised by Ana's raw anger because I knew that she
loved Lionel very much and that she knew he couldn't help himself.
We talked through the situation a bit and I promised to pray for her,
especially for the gift of patience.

Months later I got a call from a close friend of mine who also
knew Ana. She was calling about her own difficult situation of caring
for an elderly relative, but told me, without knowing I knew Ana,
that a friend named Ana had helped her immensely. She shared with
me Ana's story (for confidentiality reasons I didn't tell her that I had
spoken with Ana previously) and emphasized particularly a happy
chapter of Ana's life over the last several months. She explained that
Ana had been reading the Bible one night before going to bed and
came across the story of Jesus chiding the disciples with the imperative,
"Let the little children come to me" (Mark 10:14, NIV). Ana thought
nothing of it in the moment, but in the middle of that night she woke
up suddenly with a clear message on her mind: *Jesus loved those children
for who they were in that moment, not who they used to be or who they
would become, or what they could do for him. I need to love Lionel for who
he is now. I need to love Lionel as Jesus loves him now, as a little child.*

I started to tell my friend how beautiful the story was, but she
quickly interrupted me. "No, what's really beautiful is what Ana did

next." The next morning, I learned, Ana got up, went to Target, and bought a whiteboard with lots of colored markers—the latter because Lionel loves pens! She then asked Lionel to mount the whiteboard in the kitchen, their preferred gathering place. Then Ana began a tradition of writing down each day's schedule. She talked through with Lionel the things he always wanted to stay the same (the time they would wake up, his morning coffee, getting the mail, lunch, housework, evening news, phone calls, and bedtime) and put these in blue. She then put in red the variable weekly commitments they had together (medical appointments, visits from relatives, etc.). Finally, in green, she wrote down her own appointments that would take her out of the house.

My friend was blown away. "Ana says Jesus invited her to love Lionel, with his mental debilitation, as Jesus loved the little children. And it's working! You should see her now: it's like they're teenagers in love again. She treats him with such dignity and respect. She still gets frustrated sometimes, but there's no more anger or resentment."

I knew when I heard the story that Ana had not just learned to be kinder to Lionel. Something profoundly spiritual, supernatural, had occurred. The "clear message" she had awoken to was divine intervention. Her heart was properly disposed by her choice to read the scripture the night before (even though she probably hadn't felt very spiritual in that moment, with all the anger she had toward Lionel) and by her general openness to God being part of her life. But the story was about more than just her goodwill. It was about the God of love, the "Hound of Heaven," as the poet Francis Thompson so wonderfully wrote, who wanted her to be happy. It was about Jesus of Nazareth entering into her real-life drama and inviting her into spirit-filled living as his Junior Partner. It was also about Jesus loving Lionel. God's love for

Lionel was made manifest in a whiteboard with lots of writing instruments! It was made manifest in a wife who no longer yelled or rolled her eyes at him. It was made manifest in a calendar in the kitchen that could always clear up his confusion about what was coming next on his schedule.

Living love always starts with baby steps of human collaboration and results in a huge chain reaction of happiness. God's grace first came to Ana with a clear message in the middle of the night. She could have brushed it off. Instead, she accepted it as God's intervention in her life. She then acted on the message and made a practical resolution, using her own creativity (also a gift from God) and her knowledge of what would make Lionel happy. God sustained Ana in her work, which in turn was now helping my friend—the one who was telling me the second part of Ana's story—to love her invalid relative with renewed energy, creativity, and a supernatural spirit.

If there's one sign or mark of living love it is selflessness. Jesus's way of love was entirely selfless: "Though he was in the form of God, [he] did not count equality with God a thing to be grasped, but emptied himself, taking the form of a servant" (Phil. 2:6–7, RSV). Our new disposition is self-giving, without any demand or even desire for compensation. In relationships, the follower of Jesus is called to throw out every scale and balance. Love means gifting, donating ourselves to our neighbor in truth. When we immerse ourselves in the quasi-divine act of loving—this habit, disposition, attitude, and lifestyle of living for others for their sake—we unleash our divine likeness and are free to become everything God created us to be.

This is true for each of us. Yes, I am truly free and can become fully me when I am living detached from self and start living for you, my neighbor.

Finally, Jesus's way of love was redemptive. His "com-passion" was what he did on the cross. Jesus died willingly because his death would bring life. If he now invites us to die to ourselves and to our self-centered inclinations—with him, through living love—it is because we will also rise with him on the last day. And rise with him here and now as well, on this great earth, by experiencing the spiritual joy he wants for us! Contrary to the secular media, we are, in fact, happiest and healthiest when we are living wholly for others, confident in God's promise that he will take care of us.

The transformative disposition of living love that we're pursuing isn't simply adopting habits of niceness or philanthropy. It's imitating—indeed, partaking in—God's way of loving us. The apostle Paul couldn't have been clearer in making the distinction between good deeds and Christian love:

> Though I command languages both human and angelic—if I speak without love, I am no more than a gong booming or a cymbal clashing. And though I have the power of prophecy, to penetrate all mysteries and knowledge, and though I have all the faith necessary to move mountains—if I am without love, I am nothing. Though I should give away to the poor all that I possess, and even give up my body to be burned—if I am without love, it will do me no good whatever. (1 Cor. 13:1–3, NJB)

If all that goodness isn't love, what then is love? For St. Paul, giving all we have to the poor is not necessarily it. Not even suffering death for a good cause is a sure sign of love. It would seem, at first read, that St. Paul is saying love is not only about what we do, but also about the intentions with which we do it.

While this intentionality is an essential element of Christian love or charity, the corpus of Paul's writings and the four Gospels indicate that love is even greater than doing good things with good intentions. Christian love is me loving everyone as God loves me. Remember the New Commandment? "This is my commandment, that you love one another as I have loved you" (John 15:12, RSV).

If that's a hard concept to grasp, or if it doesn't blow your mind once you do grasp it, then you haven't experienced the quality and magnitude of God's personal and intimate love for you.

BARRIERS TO LOVE

There are all sorts of barriers that keep us from experiencing God's love. Sin is the first of these. Conversion and repentance, aided by the six self-help steps of the Make Straight the Path process (or similar steps), and culminating in God's forgiveness, remove the barrier of sin. Perhaps this is why he who has been forgiven much loves much in return.

But a clean conscience itself is not enough to experience God's love. Through my theology studies, but most of all from pastoral experience, it has become clear to me how our *capacity* to know divine love for us, in the first person, is directly related to how much *human* love has touched us.

A child who experiences abandonment in her early years, for example, almost always has a hard time accepting love later in life, at least until she is able to put her life story in the context of a world where both good and evil exist side by side. As such a person reaches adolescence, the selfless love of her adoptive parents may seem suddenly not to be enough. Seared deep into her psychology is a story of personal rejection that makes her doubt whether *any* love is real and permanent. If one experience of rejection can have such an effect, imagine how hard it is—perhaps impossible—for someone who has *never* experienced human love to experience and accept divine, perfect love at any stage of life.

But that's not to say it's ever too late to learn to love and be loved—first among mortals, then in a relationship with God. It will certainly involve making straight the path, however, as an example will illustrate.

I've had the opportunity to get to know a young man named Jerome, whose harrowing story of growing up in North Philadelphia in the late 1990s is the closest I've ever heard of a loveless existence. In 2006, the year Jerome should have graduated from high school, there were over four hundred homicides recorded in Philadelphia. By that time, Jerome was eighteen and had been on the streets for four years, witnessing and participating in some of that violence.

Jerome knows next to nothing of his origins. He eventually learned from police records that he was born in a parking lot to an unknown woman who left him for dead in a garbage can. His first weeks of life were spent in a detox facility for newborns. By the age of ten, Jerome had lived in thirteen foster homes and two institutions. His one "stable" living situation was from the ages of ten to twelve, years he spent in the home of a foster father who convinced Jerome he was his uncle and therefore it was only right that they should have a very "special" relationship. During those two years, "Uncle Evon" repeatedly molested Jerome and used him as a drug runner. In these years of pre-pubescent transition, Jerome says he learned violence as a form of self-defense and as an emotional release from the hatred he felt toward, in his words, "every living human being." Uncle Evon introduced Jerome to alcohol from their first days together, and by the age of twelve Jerome craved alcohol in the morning as an escape from feeling stupid among his peers. His youthful alcohol dependence eventually led to his being kicked out of school in the ninth grade, and he never returned.

Needless to say, Jerome followed a typical trajectory over the next few years for young men with that sort of background. He did various stints in jail (time he recalls as being the most peaceful of his first nineteen years of life) and bounced around from one temporary living situation to another, collecting unemployment while dealing and doing drugs. During all these years, Jerome never had real contact with a religious person, and he certainly had no religious training. His only contact with things spiritual, he told me, was his regular mocking of prisoners who read the Bible (a reaction that grew in part out of envy, for Jerome didn't know how to read) and the time he punched out the Protestant prison chaplain for pushing "stupid stuff." Jerome was more than happy to get a few more months for the badge of honor the chaplain episode earned him.

The turning point for Jerome, and the reason we can talk about him today, came as unexpectedly as the "clear message" came in the night to Ana. The difference? Jerome's message had nothing to do with a personal moment of "enlightenment" or "inspiration"—he wouldn't have recognized inspiration if it had knocked him down—but rather in the form of a generous and courageous soul who was already immersed in living love.

Jerome now describes John as "the first guy I ever met who wanted good things to happen to me." "Everyone else wanted my ass," he would say, with a big and contagious smile he'd tried out for the first time just two years prior. John's background was not all that different from Jerome's. The difference for John was a mother who'd genuinely loved him from day one, even if she didn't know how to raise a child. When John sobered up from his own alcohol and drug abuse, he retreated to his mom, who encouraged him to enter the military. Finally, as a soldier, he developed enough discipline to start making some good decisions. John met a low-key evangelical minister on base who saw in him great potential and took him on as his part-time assistant. John had never picked up the Bible before, but just spending time with this minister and seeing how he treated everyone spurred an interest in him in all things spiritual.

Upon finishing his military commitment, John felt a strong call to go back to his North Philadelphia neighborhood and help young people get off the street. He started a nonprofit organization that partnered with small businesses to employ in simple, part-time jobs men and women who were ready to transition from public shelters to personal residences and who needed an opportunity to establish a positive entry on an otherwise troubling résumé. When John met Jerome in March of 2009, John was calling himself a "born-again Christian," having found purpose and meaning for his life through a personal relationship with God.

John and Jerome met serendipitously, sort of. Jerome remembers perfectly that sweltering Thursday in July. He was flying high on drugs (as he was most days), but as always he was just lucid enough not to get taken advantage of by his street competitors. John was making his rounds, surveying the neighborhood, and approached Jerome on one of the younger man's preferred streetcorners. Jerome recalls John's first words to him: "I love you, man. I used to work this same corner, and I'm sure you're a good man somewhere deep down. I was a good man too; I just didn't know it at the time, because nobody believed in me and I didn't believe in myself. If you ever want to talk sometime, let me know." Jerome responded with a string of cusswords and a warning to John to stay out of his life.

Believe it or not, that encounter was the genesis of a great friendship.

John knew that Jerome had responded in the only way he knew how. That night John went to bed thinking of Jerome, wondering where he would sleep that night (divine inspiration?) and determined to pursue him with relentless kindness. From the next day forward, John looked for Jerome whenever he was in the neighborhood, and he always offered him a kind word or a bottle of water. Eventually, Jerome accepted a few hot sandwiches too, though he initially refused food because he considered handouts to be beneath him. One day, John realized he hadn't seen Jerome in over a week, and he began to ask around. He first checked with the local precinct to see if the younger man had been arrested. Nothing. Eventually, John found Jerome in a local hospital, where he had been admitted after being stabbed multiple times by another dealer in another neighborhood.

"When I saw John walk into my hospital room," Jerome told me, "a deep sense of warmth filled my whole body. I'd never felt anything like it before. It was my first real, positive connection with another human being. The moment I saw him at this low, low time of my life, I knew this guy was for real. He looked for me, he found me, and yet he didn't want anything from me. And, thank God, he didn't preach to me either!"

The more genuine human love that surrounds us, the more open we will be to the love of God whenever and however God reveals his love for us. And yet the wonderful thing about love is that we don't have to wait for it to come to us. We can love even if our loved ones don't love us in return. In fact, our love is sometimes purest when we don't get anything in return.

When Jerome got out of the hospital, he went directly to jail on more drug charges. John visited him often and, in time, shared with him his own faith journey. Jerome remained apparently aloof, telling John that the only reason he was talking to this would-be mentor was the cigarette money John would sometimes give him. John knew better: he saw the action of the Holy Spirit working on Jerome in the quiet of his heart. Most notably, Jerome started looking out for the weaker inmates protectively, and he expressed his disgust at the way some of the guys were treated.

One day Jerome shocked John by asking him about Jesus. The question was simple and honest, in typical Jerome fashion: "Who the hell does that Jesus dude think he is?" John saw the question as a crack in Jerome's armor against God and religion. "Why the hell do you care who that dude thinks he is?" retorted John, cracking a smile as he pushed back against Jerome's stern cover. The conversation ended there, but Jerome's search for the face of Jesus was just beginning. Over the next six months Jerome started taking classes to get his high school general equivalency diploma (GED), and he used the Bible as his reading text.

Jerome's friendship with John was enough to make him open more generally to friendship, or at least to healthy acquaintance, with other people. The guards quickly began to trust Jerome as one of the inmates on the good side. They gave him privileges in return for his watching their backs. These may sound like little things, but Jerome describes them as life-transforming.

The more Jerome learned to trust people, the more open he was to the love of God. Over a period of three months, Jerome devoured the New Testament. This is not to say Jerome was a new man altogether. Six months into that particular one-year sentence, Jerome got into a fight with another inmate, whom Jerome described as a "pompous SOB who had it coming." That may or may not have been true, but Jerome was the first to admit he hadn't lived up to his new values. His old habits of anger and retaliation had gotten the best of him.

The extra weeks in prison as punishment for bad behavior turned out to be a blessing, however. John had extra time to prepare himself for the big challenge of freedom. At the time, John and I didn't know each other, but the combination of John's street experience, his deep understanding of human nature, and his profound belief in and love for God naturally led him to help Jerome make the trek through our six Make Straight the Path steps, even if they weren't in this order or described in these terms.

As you read through these steps again, try to put yourself in Jerome's shoes. Identify for Jerome what each step would look like in practice. Answer out loud, or write down on paper, a description of what he would need to do. Don't do this as if you were counseling him; do it as if you were Jerome. Say what *you* are going to do.

This exercise is beneficial even if your situation is much simpler than Jerome's, because it will help you be honest with yourself as you confront the complexity of your own issues—complex, from your perspective, mostly because they are *yours*. As you do this, be especially attentive to how the Make Straight the Path process prepares you for living love.

While these six steps are mostly about basic human justice in a person's relationship to others, they clear the playing field of obstacles that would otherwise make it impossible to live as spirit-filled men and women who live for others, for their own sake, in the mode of Jesus of Nazareth.

Make Straight the Path

1. Make a searching and fearless moral inventory of your life.

2. Admit to God, to yourself, and to other human beings the exact nature of your wrongs and your powerlessness over them.

3. Turn your will over to God's care and live trusting that he can make you whole.

4. Begin to live the New Commandment: "Love one another as I have loved you."

5. Make amends to anyone you have harmed along the way with your selfish pursuits.

6. Design and follow a practical plan to hold yourself accountable to God and to others.

Jerome is now studying at a community college and in a carpenter's apprentice program in another city in the Northeast. Most important, he's trying to be for others what John was for him. I have no doubt Jerome will continue to grow in his love for God and for others as he develops character, on the one hand, and as he lets the theological virtue of love transform his heart.

We know what that transformation looks like. It is living love. When the theological virtue of charity reigns in our heart, we become the hands and feet of Christ for our friends and enemies. When love has enveloped our personality, our natural sense for survival and self-protection expands slowly, then quickly, to include looking out for the survival and well-being of every member of God's family. Our ever-enduring ego is transformed by love from a bullhorn that reminds us to look out for number one into a whole orchestra of the soul, its glorious sound filling our heart with aspirations for justice and mercy for all.

As this happens, as we collaborate with God's grace and begin to love others as God loves us and them, we are replacing selfishness with a lifestyle of living love.

The process of forging living love is different for everyone. Perhaps you know people who seem to have been born thinking of others and looking out for their concerns. There's a man in my parish named Joe who's that way; he goes about doing good. His quick smile is the visible reflection of his servant's heart. He is unassuming in his service and disinterested in petty disputes. If you need something done and nobody else wants to do it, you go to Joe. He'll do it for no other reason than his love for making others happy. For him, charity is a disposition of the heart that has overtaken his thoughts and his desires. It is this habit of genuine charity of the heart that we call living love.

Then we shift our focus from someone like Joe and look at ourselves, and we see more selfishness than living love. We're tempted to give up or to keep our charity engines in neutral, preferring circumstances to dictate whether we move forward or backward in our imitation of Christ. But living love isn't just for the naturally meek and humble. Charity is the true sign of *any* Christian. It is God's only measuring stick. As such, no matter what personality type we have and no matter what our cultural background, we all have the same mission: to learn to love. St. Augustine had it right: "Love and do what you will."

Have you ever wondered what God will say to you when you meet him face to face at the hour of your death? I think about it often, and I try to recall one scripture passage in particular. There is only one place in the Bible that specifically describes what the Final Judgment will be like. It's in the Gospel of Matthew. Read these verses slowly and let them sink in. It's Jesus telling us what God asks of us in this life:

> When the Son of Man comes in his glory, and all the angels with him, then he will sit on the throne of his glory. All the nations will be gathered before him, and he will separate people one from one another as a shepherd separates the sheep from the goats, and he will put the sheep at his right hand and the goats at the left. Then the king will say to those at his right hand, "Come, you that are blessed by my Father, inherit the kingdom prepared for you from the foundation of the world; for I was hungry and you gave me food, I was thirsty and you gave me something to drink, I was a stranger and you welcomed me, I was naked and you gave me clothing, I was sick and you took care of me, I was in prison and you visited me." Then the righteous will answer him, "Lord, when was it that we saw you hungry and gave you food, or thirsty and gave you something to drink? And when was it that we saw you a stranger and welcomed you, or naked and gave you clothing? And when was it that we saw you sick or in prison and visited you?" And the king will answer them, "Truly I tell you, just as you did it to one of the least of these who are members of my family, you did it to me." Then he will say to those at his left hand, "You that are accursed, depart from me into the eternal fire prepared for the devil and his angels; for I was hungry and you gave me no food, I was thirsty and you gave me nothing to drink, I was a stranger and you did not welcome me, naked and you did not give me clothing, sick and in prison and you did not visit me. . . . Truly I tell you, just as you did not do it

to one of the least of these, you did not do it to me." And these will go away into eternal punishment, but the righteous into eternal life. (Matt. 25:31–46, NRSV)

Rather than *speaking* more about love, let's learn from a man whom I respect as a great and holy lover of humanity, even if he never came to know or accept publicly the grace of Jesus Christ.

I find Mahatma Gandhi's life an example of particular importance to our journey toward living love, because like no other public non-Christian of our time, Gandhi understood charity as a gift of self to another for that person's own sake. Not only did he make no distinction between persons, but he explained his love for them as a response to the inherent dignity they possessed.

I invite you to recall his life and work in the paragraphs below, in the context of what God is asking of *you* in very different circumstances.

MAHATMA GANDHI: AN EXAMPLE OF LIVING LOVE

You have probably already pictured him in your mind: a small, frail, shriveled man dressed in a white *dhoti,* the traditional dress of Indian men. This is the image of Mahatma Gandhi that Ben Kingsley and the award-winning film *Gandhi* have imprinted within our collective mind. Gandhi is known as the father of modern-day India, having led the oppressed Indians during the first half of the twentieth century to cast off imperial British rule and gain Indian independence via nonviolent means.

But to focus on his political achievements is really to miss the essence of the man and the extraordinary, unique example he provided.

Gandhi said this about politics: "If I seem to take part in politics, it is only because politics encircles us today like the coil of a snake from which one cannot get out, no matter how much one tries. I wish therefore to wrestle with the snake."

Politics was neither his goal nor the preferred means of reaching his goal, which was social reform that would respect the dignity of every person. Gandhi's philosophy ultimately had implications that demanded a shakeup of the political world. He saw the need for politics to operate in the service of the common good and thus presented a reformed politics throughout his campaign for "character-building" in India. "My work of social reform was in no way less or subordinate to political work," Gandhi wrote. In 1931, after a successful political campaign, he said:

> The fact is that when I saw that to a certain extent my social
> work would be impossible without the help of political work,
> I took to the latter and only to the extent that it helped the
> former. I must therefore confess that work of social reform or
> self-purification of this nature is a hundred times dearer to me
> than what is called purely political work.

What motivated and shaped the underlying philosophy and work of this man? Gandhi provides insight when he says, "My life is one indivisible whole, and all my activities run into one another, and they all have their rise in my insatiable love of mankind." It is with sheer practicality rather than conscious humility that he casts off the praise of admirers, for his entire point is that nothing he does is extraordinary; rather, he argues, it is completely within the powers of every single human person:

I have not conceived my mission to be that of a knight-errant wandering everywhere to deliver people from difficult situations. My humble occupation has been to show people how they can solve their own difficulties. . . . My work will be finished if I succeed in carrying conviction to the human family, that every man or woman, however weak in body, is the guardian of his or her self-respect and liberty.

Mahatma Gandhi was extraordinary because he saw that "being the change you wish to see in the world" was the only way to achieve lasting social change. In other words, it is our own conversion that will effect societal transformation.

Gandhi's famous activist methods of noncooperation and non-violence grew from his acute awareness of the human person and the person's relation to genuine transformation. This transformation is a process of *conversion* rather than *compulsion*. And conversion requires that an oppressor come to an *understanding* of the errors of his ways. The only way to assist him in this is by demonstrating one's own dignity—by proving that one is the master of one's own will—in a patient manner that seeks the mutual good of the oppressor and oneself.

Thus, Gandhi developed a concept called *satyagraha,* the notion of soul-force, where the conquest of the adversary comes through adopting suffering in one's own person. Evoking the words of Christ to love one's enemies as oneself (and of course evoking Christ's self-sacrificial example), Gandhi explained that *satyagraha* is a method rooted in love, the most compelling force that exists.

It is because of this philosophy that the struggle for Indian independence retained a nonviolent character. Physical force was forbidden, for no matter the circumstances, it would violate the dignity of the opponent and be a response of hatred that seeks power, not a response rooted in love. *Satyagraha* seeks a solution that is authentically and mutually good for all of humankind. Gandhi was careful to insist that this is markedly different from passive resistance, for *satyagraha* involves strong and attacking actions, not passivity; however, the objects of attack must be measures and systems, never human beings.

Mahatma Gandhi is a spiritual hero because he recognized the spiritual basis within the human person and its link to a higher order or law of God. When the world order failed to align with the order of God, Gandhi showed how spiritual force—the means by which a person takes on suffering in order to witness to the importance and significance of his or her convictions—can provide the most compelling witness to truth and begin the process of conversion in hearts and consciences.

Gandhi considered every human being deserving of an authentic and equal response of love, whether they were Indian or British, Hindu or Muslim, members of the highest or lowest Hindu castes. In India, he remains a controversial figure to this day for suggesting that the very concept of "untouchability," the lowest position within the caste system, is incommensurate with the reality of the human person, and for demanding that the political and social systems change accordingly.

A little-known element of Gandhi's charity deserves more attention than it gets. Throughout his life, Gandhi made several statements against a notion of charity as indiscriminate alms-giving. "My *ahimsa* [nonviolent approach]," Gandhi said, "would not tolerate the idea of giving a free meal to a healthy person who has not worked for it in some honest way, and if I had the power, I would stop every *sadavrata* where free meals are given. It has degraded the nation and it has encouraged laziness, idleness, hypocrisy and even crime."

Gandhi understood that charity is not about financial giving; true charity rests upon the end to which the giving is directed. If giving occurs out of selfish motivation or even toward an end that does not authentically help a person, it cannot be called true charity. If giving encourages a person to continue a life of laziness or dependence, it is not helping him to realize his full potential and build his own character, and thus it entrenches him within a spiral of poverty and degradation.

Mahatma Gandhi famously chided Christians for being so unlike Jesus Christ. He said, "I like your Christ, I do not like your Christians. Your Christians are so unlike your Christ."

Given those words, I can't help but wonder what a great follower of Jesus Christ Gandhi might have become if he had met more Christians living love! What would he have thought, for example, of Mother Teresa of Calcutta, who worked for much of the twentieth century with the poorest of the poor in Gandhi's beloved India? Mother Teresa was just beginning her work when Gandhi died. I'm confident he became her biggest fan from his new vantage point.

Some would argue that Gandhi did just fine without Jesus—he was a good man who did great things. I couldn't agree more. I would say he did amazingly well without Jesus. His natural goodness and the fruits of his work serve as a beacon that proclaims to a highly diverse world the universal capacity of human reason to know, in big strokes, what is right and wrong, and the strength of the human soul to stand for good and fight evil at great personal cost.

The goal we set out for ourselves in this book, however, goes beyond learning natural goodness. It involves reaching for beatitude—supernatural happiness found through union with God, through his son Jesus Christ—and becoming everything God created us to be. Doing good, even lots of good, is a great start, but we were made for so much more. We were made to flourish on all levels in preparation for eternal life.

How many good people are out there who are still searching for transcendent meaning in life? How many philanthropists are wondering if there is something more than fixing the here and now? How many spiritual souls are thirsting for answers? Perhaps they are looking for the very thing Mahatma Gandhi bemoaned never having seen: true Christian witness, ordinary people like you and me who might dare take Christ at his word: "I have come that you might have life—life in abundance!" (John 10:10, paraphrase).

Another part of the healing of our will through love happens when we see the personal blessings we receive from our self-giving. We begin to love loving, not only because it benefits others (our first intention), but also because we recognize that this way of life makes us happier, healthier people. The two intentions are not contradictory, because they are both in line with God's will for us. We love others because they deserve to be loved for their own sake, and through our loving action, God is loving us back. Ironically—or, perhaps better said, according to God's mysterious logic—the more we give ourselves away, the more we find ourselves. It is in giving up self that we recover self, not only as it was before we gave it up, but as God has always meant our souls to be, glorious human images of his divinity.

WE HAVE NOW outlined the Faith-Hope-Love Cure. If we are looking for a miracle in our lives, we don't have to look further. God's choice miracle is grace. Grace is "Emmanuel, God with us"—Jesus—and he lives within us as faith, hope, and love.

There is no reason to worry if *knowing* the Faith-Hope-Love Cure has not yet made you whole. Our spiritual life is a journey that involves head knowledge, but it is primarily about bringing this knowledge from the head down to the heart, where we welcome God as the sweet guest of our soul; there he dwells within us every day and every hour and in every one of our relationships. In heaven this won't be *work*. Until then, every moment is a new beginning, a new chance to collaborate with the Divine Cure.

The forthcoming chapter is an invitation to dive into that cure. It is meant as inspiration to embark upon or go further in the adventure of *living faith, living hope,* and *living love.* The human project of building a worthy and happy life is always complex and sometimes messy. Whether you're going through very difficult times now or are stuck in your daily routine without much inspiration, here are concrete and powerful ways to become everything God created you to be.

PART 3

The Program

CHAPTER 8

Living Saints: Bringing It Home

Among the many wonderful parts of being a priest is the chance to comfort people in the throes of tragedy. Like pastors and clerics of many religious traditions, I visit the sick, bury the dead, console survivors and victims, and mediate conflict. Although it is difficult at times to be so often and intimately involved in emotional and physical trauma, almost without exception I come away from these experiences with renewed hope in God and in the human spirit.

This hope is not easy to explain. In fact, the greatest argument against the existence of an all-loving and all-powerful God is precisely the fact that hope is necessary. If God were to keep us from suffering, if he always intervened and made us well, if heaven were on earth, we wouldn't need faith or trust. The argument is a strong one: Why does God make things so difficult for his children?

If there is no rational, acceptable answer to that question, if God does not offer us a way forward, out of natural or self-inflicted messes, I would have to agree that Christianity is a big farce. I certainly wouldn't put my trust in a God who had no answer to real human suffering.

But there *is* a way forward. I believe that the Faith-Hope-Love Cure—the Divine Cure—is God's usual way of healing us from within from every one of our ailments. No matter what comes our way, if we allow God to dwell within us through the theological virtues, nothing can defeat us. Some days will feel worse than others, our lives or the lives of our loved ones may even be cut short here on earth, but with faith, hope, and love we will not despair because we know God is always at our side. As we pass through this imperfect world and get our bumps and bruises, we do so with joy and meaning, knowing that God has something wonderful waiting for us just around the corner, both on earth and in heaven.

THE FAITH-HOPE-LOVE CURE IN ACTION

In other parts of this book, I have changed the names or circumstances of individuals to protect their privacy. I would now, however, like to introduce you to Cynthia Mernagh of Akron, Ohio. I have asked her permission to narrate her story and use her name because she's the greatest testimony I have ever witnessed of living faith, living hope, and living love. Her story needs to be told. Her life is a testament to the Divine Cure and its power to make us profoundly happy, no matter what life brings our way.

Cynthia is married to Dan, and together they have eight children. Six years ago Cynthia was diagnosed with an advanced stage of breast cancer. Her children were between five and nineteen years old at the time.

When I was a cynical teenager I knew "Mrs. Mernagh" mostly as the lady from the neighborhood who always expressed euphoric joy about things I considered to be altogether ordinary and even boring. I can still hear her high-pitched greeting as she entered my house, or welcomed us into hers. For the hundredth time she would tell me and my older brother how *wonderful* it was to see us. Joe and I had no interest in greeting any of my mom's friends, but Mrs. Mernagh, with all of that enthusiasm directed at us, was to be avoided especially.

Looking back now on our contact with Mrs. Mernagh, one thing stands out: we knew that her joy was genuine. Although we responded to her kindness with rolled eyes and devious chuckles, we knew this woman was real.

Now we know just how real and holy she was and is. After several years of remission, Cynthia's cancer returned and has now metastasized. It is in her spine, pelvis, lungs, and skull. In this crucible of physical and emotional suffering, Cynthia has shown everyone around her what it means to be a Christian, displaying the miracle of grace God can perform in a willing and generous soul.

A couple of months ago, Cynthia shared with a group of women in the neighborhood her situation in these terms:

Despite radiation and several rounds of chemotherapy, my cancer continues to spread. This shows me that life can be full of surprises and changes, and emphasizes the reality that we are not ultimately living for this life alone. Each day, I must ask, "What is it that you want from me today, Lord? How is it that I can best complete your will?" I must resist the temptation to be afraid or to play in my imagination the scenario for my children of "life without Mom." I have only each day to love God, to love Dan, and to love my children and others. That's my mission right now. In reality, I suppose that this has always been my mission.

In just a few sentences, Cynthia describes for us the Divine Cure. I have been so deeply moved by her life with cancer that I asked if she would be willing to go into more detail with me as a contribution to this book. Specifically, I told her I wanted her to tell us what faith, hope, and love mean for her, now that she knows she's dying and leaving her husband and children behind.

The day I was to speak with Cynthia she began to experience new difficulty in motor skills, and her doctor ordered her back in for more tests. She was also very tired. But her last e-mail to me, in response to my suggestion that maybe we should delay our conversation because of these complications, says it all: "9:30 A.M. it is!!" I doubt that Cynthia wrote those exclamation marks because she *felt* like talking at 9:30 A.M. She wrote them because she *willed passionately* to do the right thing.

Keep in mind as you listen to Cynthia that she has already made straight the path of the Lord. It is evident from her approach to life and death that there are no major issues she has avoided dealing with. I find with most people that some significant issue from the past stands in the way of experiencing God's grace as Cynthia does. God can still give a person a level of peace in difficult times, but the issues that have never been cleared away, either through the six Make Straight the Path steps or through the process of getting unstuck (as described in chapter 3), stop the mighty flow of grace from sweeping in and taking over our soul, as it obviously has done for Cynthia.

What follows is a window into our conversation. As you read Cynthia's responses, I invite you to think back on how we defined *living faith, living hope,* and *living love.* This is what such habits look like in one person in very difficult circumstances. But Cynthia didn't form the habits when she got sick; they were a way of life for her dating back at least as long as I've known her. The Faith-Hope-Love Cure isn't just for sick people, but seeing what those theological virtues have done in and for this good woman is an inspiration for all of us to make them get a hold of us beginning today.

FATHER JONATHAN: Cynthia, what does faith mean to you now?

CYNTHIA: It's just knowing God as my Father who loves me. And knowing too that his love for me doesn't depend on what I do or don't do. For example, he doesn't love me less or more now that I'm sick. I can trust in him because his love for me is like this.

FATHER JONATHAN: What about hope?

CYNTHIA: It would be hard for me to imagine life without the ultimate hope of someday arriving in heaven. Also, hope is confidence in the fact that my suffering will bring about good for others.

FATHER JONATHAN: But how would your suffering help someone else?

CYNTHIA: Well, for example, one of my children was going through a hard time, and so I told Jesus, "You can let my cancer come back and I'll offer that up for the sake of my child; I will unite my suffering to the suffering of Christ." One week later we found out that my cancer was back. So I know I can bring life to others. That's my mission right now.

Another example is I have a niece who is suffering anorexia, so when I don't feel like eating because I'm so sick, I eat for her. This is a little sacrifice I offer up to Jesus.

FATHER JONATHAN: But what does your eating have to do with her eating?

CYNTHIA: Well, I naturally think of her when I don't feel like eating, so I know Jesus understands that when I go ahead and eat (that's what the doctors want me to do), God will give her a special grace. I'm trying to do for her what she can't do for herself because of her sickness.

That reminds me: I think there's so much suffering going to waste in the world. Offering up my suffering as a prayer is my mission. It's the tool that I have. I even offer up my suffering for things like the economy and this recession we're in, for people to get jobs. When Jesus was suffering on the cross and prayed for us, don't you think his prayer was especially effective?

FATHER JONATHAN: *I know you're awfully tired these days. Do you ever feel too tired to pray? Do you actually say prayers in full sentences? How do you pray?*

CYNTHIA: *That's a very good question, because if I relied on my own memory to remember what prayers to say, I couldn't pray at all these days. I trust that the good Lord knows my heart. I don't have to say sentences or even words. I'm just connected with him and he reads my heart.*

FATHER JONATHAN: *What does love mean for you? How do you practice it?*

CYNTHIA: *Oh, well, I'm sorry if I repeat myself here. Faith, hope, and love are just so interconnected for me. I say to the Lord, "This cancer was your idea. This is your gift to me. I hope I do a good job carrying it." That's how I try to love God: by carrying my cross the best I can.*

We've taken on a little family motto. It goes like this—it's just three lines, so it's easy for me to remember: "Remember the past with gratitude, live the present with passion, and look to the future with confidence."

Living the present with passion is my favorite. Although I'm tempted to fear what will happen to the children when I'm no longer here, I've decided that such fear just keeps me from living the present with passion. So, for example, last week I started volunteering at my church. I'm working in the sacristy getting the altar and everything ready, and cleaning. Dan and I were a little bit worried when I started because we don't know how long I'll be able to keep the job, but I thought, "I'm still alive right now, so we don't have to worry about how long I can do it."

Again, the real temptation is to start wondering what things will be like for Phillip, for example, who is only twelve years old. But we've decided as a family that we're going to pedal this bicycle together. We aren't going to worry. We're just going to keep on pedaling.

FATHER JONATHAN: Is there any one thought that helps you stay so strong?

CYNTHIA: Well, there's one scripture passage that means a lot to me. It's Hebrews 10:35–36. I especially like the first part. It says, "Surrender not your confidence, for it has a great reward." The rest of it goes like this: "For you have need of endurance, so that when you have done the will of God, you may receive what was promised." So that's what I say to myself when I take my daughter out to practice for her driving test: "The Lord is in charge; don't surrender!" Or the same when I'm taking care of Andrew. [Andrew is my uncle. He has special needs and has been living with Cynthia and Dan for several years.] God only shows us so much, so we have to just keep going and trust in God our Father, who loves immensely, no matter what we can do or can't do.

Before saying goodbye, Cynthia invited me to come visit them the next time I'm in Ohio. In her words, "It would be *wonderful* to see you!" and she meant it now just as she did when I was a teenager. This time I got it. Sadly, Cynthia passed away a few weeks after our interview.

Cynthia was grateful for the past, she lived the present with passion, and even as she was dying, she looked to the future with confidence. Because she collaborated with God's grace, the Faith-Hope-Love Cure kept her from defining herself as a sick person, or as a mother who was about to leave her husband and children, or as a victim of an undeserved disease.

Instead, she saw herself for who she really was: a daughter of a loving Father who knew her suffering, was on her side, and would be faithful to his promise to bring about a greater good out of all of this suffering. Faith healed her intellect by freeing her from shallowness—she perceived supernatural truth. Hope healed her memory by freeing her from fearful thoughts of all the terrible things that could possibly occur. And love healed her will by freeing her from self-centeredness and allowing her to live her days focused on the people and God whom she loves. Cynthia was deeply happy, and that's evidence of the Divine Cure.

Because I know the Mernagh family, I already know what greater good God may be bringing forth from the tragedy of Cynthia's illness. One little piece of that good is that six of the eight Mernagh children have decided they want to become missionaries and are already studying to accomplish this dream (five of the boys are studying to be priests!) Their love for God started long before their mother's sickness, but it was the faith, hope, and love they found in the home—in the good times *and* in the bad—that gave them the vision and desire to do something big for God, their loving Father, and for others. Listen to what Cynthia told me about raising her children:

From the outset of our marriage, Dan and I desired to raise our children to love and serve the Lord. What was most important to us, our individual relationship with the Lord, was what we most desired to pass on to our children. What good would it be if they succeeded in many areas, if they enjoyed many material possessions, if they won the acclaim of others—what would any of this matter apart from the joy of personally knowing and loving the Lord?

A relationship with Christ is a gift, and, like a vocation, is one that only the Lord can give. Understanding this, we strove to put our children in the best position to receive this gift.

If Christ were at the center of their lives, then we knew that whatever vocation to which they were called would be lived to the full.

So Dan and I determined that we would work hard to fulfill what we saw as the main job that we had as parents: helping our children discover their own vocations and preparing them to live these. One of the best ways that we could do this was to provide a stable marriage and family life for the children. Dan and I had observed many family situations where disunity between parents, lack of forgiveness or affection, financial stress, anger, or serious sins resulted in grown children struggling with poor self-esteem and the inability to make prudent decisions. By contrast, a secure home environment provides for emotionally healthy and secure children. It gives them the confidence to launch themselves "out into the deep" to follow Christ's call for their lives and to face life in general.

Maybe you feel a long way away from living the Faith-Hope-Love Cure as Cynthia and Dan have done it. The good news is we don't have to be like Cynthia and Dan. Just as Cynthia says to the Lord, "This cancer was your idea. This is your gift to me. I hope I do a good job carrying it," so we can thank the Lord, in our own words and ways, for permitting the particular sufferings in our life, no matter what they are. All we have to concern ourselves with is "doing a good job carrying it," as Cynthia said. Carrying our cross well will look very different for each of us. We may not sound as spiritual as Cynthia did or think such spiritual thoughts. But if we're going to allow God to have his way with us through the Divine Cure, we can rely on the enduring truths on which faith, hope, and love depend. These truths do not change.

Think, for example, of Cynthia's great hope in heaven. Where did she get that? She got it from the Bible. She got it from the church. She got it from prayer. It's a divine promise God made to us thousands of years ago. And it's personal: there will come a time in our existence, not long from now, when God will look at us knowingly and lovingly, embrace us as his prodigal children, and wipe away every one of our tears.

Perfectly aware of the heart-wrenching cause of each of our tears, tuned in to the highly personal, backstage drama that provoked them, our loving Father will make our tears go away forever—if we let him—and will fill our heart to the brim with beatitude, contentment, and joy.

This spiritual journey starts with God-help (we have been loved by God, he has given us life, and he sustains us), it continues with self-help (using the natural mechanisms God has given us of intelligence and will), and it is brought to fruition through more God-help, in the form of faith, hope, and love.

SOAK YOURSELF IN SPIRITUAL TRUTH

No matter the degree of divine life we have developed in our interior, we can make it grow by reflecting on God's Word:

> And [God] will wipe away every tear from their eyes; and there will no longer be any death; there will no longer be any mourning, or crying, or pain; the first things have passed away. (Rev. 21:4, NASB)

Every day holds out to us a choice between shallowness and living faith, between fear and living hope, between self-centeredness and living love. We can rely solely on our intelligence and moods to tell us whether or not we should be happy, based on temporal and changing circumstances (many of which we have no control over), or we can enrich our reason, memory, and will with spiritual truth and start counting on God's master plan for our happiness.

Doing this requires meditating on the Word of God. It requires opening our eyes and seeking out what God may have to say about our situation, even if we don't understand it yet.

It takes only a moment to make a leap of faith into the supernatural realm. Remembering that God's plan encompasses both our eternal salvation and our earthly happiness (beatitude), we can say a prayer like this:

> Jesus, some things don't look so good today. In fact, I'm
> tempted to think everything looks bad. I don't know how
> things will turn out. But I do know the end of the story. You
> and I, and the people I love, will win. Every one of my tears,
> and the tears of my loved ones, will be wiped away. I believe
> in you. I love you. Today I will do my part.

The specific words don't matter. If the above words don't suit your circumstances, say any other prayer of praise and commitment, from the heart.

Thousands of years before that beautiful verse from the book of Revelation—the above-quoted verse about wiping away our tears—and still hundreds of years before Jesus's birth, the prophet Isaiah foretold our encounter with this merciful and all-loving God. Isaiah describes divine consolation of our pain as even more than the wiping away of tears. He says God will care for us with the tenderness of a mother who nurses her child: "As nurslings, you shall be carried in her arms, and fondled in her lap; as a mother comforts her child, so will I comfort you" (Isa. 66:13, NAB).

Today we can either wallow in our emotional wounds or enjoy the passion of now and confidence in tomorrow. We can stay on the surface or we can go deep and imagine the fabulous future that awaits us. This isn't just positive thinking; it's spiritual mind-management that syncs our brain and emotions with truth. It is discerning which thoughts are of God (the ones that invite us to be more like him) and which thoughts are useless, at best, and more likely temptations of Satan, who wants us stuck in the past, sad, and hopeless. It is regulating which thoughts have permission to stick around and which ones we'll tell to keep on moving because they aren't from God.

THE FAITH-HOPE-LOVE CURE IN OUR DAILY ROUTINE

While life's most difficult moments can be tipping points that challenge us to go from good to great in our spiritual life, as we saw in the last chapter, we don't have to wait for exceptional times to be transformed by the Faith-Hope-Love Cure.

If we were ever to doubt that ordinary life can have great value, we would need only to recall that the first thirty years of Jesus's life were spent—intentionally—in obscurity. He lived with his parents, worked as a carpenter's apprentice, and worked no known miracles. These years were not mere preparation for important things he would do later; they were part of his saving work. He was living his Father's will even before he began to preach, travel, and heal.

Jesus wasn't alone in choosing such simplicity. Mary and Joseph played key roles in the history of salvation, but they did so in the quiet of their homes. The relative silence of the Gospel writers regarding Mary and Joseph makes their lives all the more powerful, for it tells us we can live the Faith-Hope-Love Cure right now in our own unexceptional circumstances.

Of course, a life of simplicity and obscurity alone doesn't make us holy or even good. In the secrecy of our conscience, we make or break who we are. Whether we are public figures or completely unknown, nothing we do or say can take the place of how well we preserve our sacred soul. We do this by living faith, living hope, and living love in our daily routine.

This section of the chapter is an invitation to continue translating our desire for self-improvement, holiness, and happiness into a life-long spiritual program. Perhaps we fear that we might not be growing fast enough or even going in the right direction. Our lives are full of activity. We don't think about spiritual things all the time, or even every day. Most of our time is spent working to pay bills, picking up the kids, doing laundry, and taking care of other routine matters. We worry about our husband and what he's doing and whether he's happy with us. We worry about how we'll get the kids through college. And amidst all of that activity, we ask ourselves whether life boils down to one big distraction.

Maybe we *are* distracted, but the good news is we don't need to run off and join a monastery to get focused on the right things. By taking human form, Jesus elevated our humanity, giving it divine dignity. God not only made our souls in his image and likeness; he made himself—Jesus—in our image, with all the complications that being human implies. The Bible tells us Jesus was like us in all things but sin. For this reason we can say with confidence that we can be like Jesus even when we're doing very mundane things. All the work of keeping ourselves financially stable, healthy, and happy can be part of our spiritual life.

Our union with God depends on how we do the things we do. There are three fabulous entrance points into the Divine Cure that we can apply in our daily routine—that is, doing the things we do:

1. Do ordinary things in an extraordinary way.

2. Let go of just causes.

3. Consult regularly with the Senior Partner.

Do Ordinary Things in an Extraordinary Way

I know a man who shines shoes on the corner of Sixth Avenue and Forty-Seventh Street in New York City. In good fun and with admirable efficiency, he whistles at, jokes with, heckles, and berates potential customers as they pass by his stand. He has turned what could be a very boring job into a happy show that makes others smile and brings him a whole lot of business too.

I know many others who make a lot more money than he does, who never have to drum up business as he does—and who don't smile half as much as he does. One day as I sat high in my friend's chair, I asked him what keeps him so happy. I asked him if he had suffered much in his life. He responded by telling me a harrowing story of personal betrayal by his former wife, the mother of his children. It happened years ago, but it still affects his daily life as he deals with a broken family.

"So why are you so happy?" I asked. "Given all that's happened, aren't you angry? With all of that in your background, how can you always be smiling and making people laugh?"

His answer surprised me for its profound simplicity. "I made a decision a long time ago not to worry about the things I can't change."

"So do you just not think about it, or what?" I persisted.

"Yes," he replied, "basically that's it. I'm not ignoring reality, but I decided I don't need to go down that road. I don't want revenge. I don't want hate. Life is what it is, and I'm moving forward. There are so many good things to be grateful to God for—why would I focus on the one thing that went really bad?"

He later revealed that he keeps a very cordial and healthy relationship with the mother of his children, for their sake, but also for his. His days are a blessing for others—including those family members—and are totally his because he hasn't let his heart wallow in self-pity or anger.

My friend didn't explain his approach in spiritual terms, but what he has chosen to do is deeply spiritual. He has protected his soul from the devil's favorite weapons of anger and resentment and has chosen to live each moment with passion and look to the future with confidence. There's a lot of faith, hope, and love there!

The difference between a life of general distraction and one of profound spirituality is actually quite small in terms of what we have to do to go from one to the other. This is because we don't get holy by doing holy things. God makes us holy by dwelling within us; all *we* have to do is invite him in through faith, hope, and love.

How many negative thoughts will run through our minds if we let them? Take a fast today from all negative thoughts and summon up positive, true thoughts to put in their place. What comes out of your mouth is what is already in your heart. Make your heart pure, and life will look better for you and everyone who comes near you. Look for the good in yourself and others, all day long. Let people around you know the good you see in them and in their actions.

Today is a blessing, and it is all yours. It is filled with opportunities of grace and life. Today you can live ordinary things at work and at home in an extraordinary way. You can choose to be fully engaged in every activity, because as a child of God everything you do, as unimportant as it may feel, has great value in your Father's eyes. The formula for a great day is incredibly simple: be aware of who you are; seek God's will in the big things and in the little things too; and do whatever you do with dedication, grace, and a smile.

Let Go of Just Causes

There is no faster entry into the Divine Cure than through culti-vating a heart of mercy in our daily routine. Forgiveness is the ultimate merit badge and the defining characteristic of a mature Christian; it is the crown jewel of personal development. No other human affair brings us closer to Jesus in his redemptive act of suffering, death, and resurrection than our free-will choice to forgive those who trespass against us.

Yesterday someone made fun of me for a gaffe I made on televi-sion. He did it in front of people whose opinions of me I admittedly care too much about. For several hours I ruminated over what he'd done. I stoked the fire of my wounded pride with useless and unchari-table thoughts about his possible intentions.

Still stuck in my pettiness, I walked by a security guard whose job it is to ensure that only authorized personnel enter certain secured areas of the building. Out of the corner of my eye I saw an important on-air personality rush through one of the doors, crashing into the security guard as he passed through. It was quite evident that the reporter knew he'd hit this gentleman—the contact was consider-able—but he expressed no apparent concern other than waving his hand over his shoulder as he scurried away, as if to show some generic regret. I went over and spoke to the security guard to make sure he was all right. He responded with these words: "I'm fine; in fact, I'm even better than before, because it's good to get humbled every once in a while." Now *that's* living faith, living hope, and living love!

Immediately I turned to God, remembering my simmering resentment over a perceived slight. "Jesus, I'm handing over to you my negative feelings," I prayed. "Forgive me for being so silly."

Practicing mercy in our daily routine brings us close to the heart of Jesus. And the more we reflect on how much mercy God has shown to us, the more we will want to show mercy to everyone around us. Think of this: God became man in the person of Jesus of Nazareth *in order to forgive us.* He came to earth *because forgiveness is that sweet*—so sweet that he was willing to be crucified by us, his own children, so he could share mercy with us.

During the Easter Vigil service in many churches throughout the world, this ancient sequence is sung: "O happy fault . . . that gained for us so great a Redeemer."

O happy fault? Yes! If it weren't for original sin, and for our personal sin, we wouldn't know the breadth and power of divine love. Nor would we know how our participation in this forgiveness can set us free from our deepest and darkest emotions of anger, resentment, and fear. Surely it would have been better never to have offended God, just as it would have been better for the Prodigal Son never to have left his father; but in God's logic, so unlike our own, what should never have happened is now transformed into an incomparable blessing. A huge debt that we could never have paid on our own has been forgiven, and now we are embraced by God as prodigal children whom he loves, not because of how good we've been or what we can do for him in the future, but only because we are his children. And because he loved us in this manner, we know what true love is and are capable of loving others in like form.

Jesus taught Christian forgiveness most perfectly as he hung from the cross and forgave his executioners and those who were behind his gruesome death (Pontius Pilate, some Jewish leaders, the disciples who betrayed him, you and me). He looked at us as we were killing him and groaned, "Forgive them, Father, for they know not what they do."

The basis of Christian forgiveness is not the leveling of the scales of justice. Forgiveness is not a calculation of sufficient payment. It is not a debt-reduction gimmick. Just the opposite is true. Christian forgiveness is letting go of a just cause we rightly have against someone. It is burning the accounts-receivable file and going right back into friendship and love with people whom, because of our selfless love, we see no longer as our debtors, and as if they never were.

Forgiveness is a decision of the will to let go, completely, and only out of love. What about forgiving someone who refuses to ask for forgiveness? What about forgiving someone who doesn't want to be forgiven? What about forgiving someone who doesn't think she's done anything wrong? Yes, yes, and yes. Radical forgiveness of this type, day in and day out, will move us quickly into the Divine Cure, where we accept at the core of our existence that our happiness doesn't depend on anyone treating us well, but rather on union with God, who has forgiven us of much more than anyone owes us.

Consult Regularly with the Senior Partner

We spoke in the first chapter of this book about our role as Junior Partners of the Holy Spirit. God has chosen to depend on us for his work of salvation, charity, and justice. We are his hands and feet in a world dying of a lack of love.

In our daily routine we can be Junior Partners by forming a habit of regular consultation with the Holy Spirit. We can do this not just when we find ourselves in a predicament, but rather as we plan and execute each and every day.

Start out your morning with prayer. The outline for Christian meditation I offered in an earlier chapter is one method. But no matter how you pray, make sure you talk to Jesus about the things that weigh on your heart. What are your concerns for the day? Write them down. What do you have to accomplish? Make a list. Set a plan. Present the plan in prayer to your Senior Partner, the Holy Spirit, and ask him if he has any items for you to add to your agenda. Now alter your plan accordingly. His concern for your day is bigger than yours. His resources are infinite, and he places them all at your disposal.

Are you anxious about a meeting? Take time, in prayer, to figure out why. Ask yourself probing questions. Does that person you're meeting with make you feel insecure? Is it his tone of voice, his haughty demeanor, his questioning of your motives? The Holy Spirit will surely tell you that attitude is his problem only, and it doesn't make you any better or worse in God's eyes. Let it go. Turn instead to the One who made you, because he willed you here on this earth, and he accompanies you today as you set forth.

Our consultation with our Senior Partner, our loving Father, doesn't end when our morning prayer is over. Throughout the day we're constantly making decisions. Whenever there's a decision of consequence, don't go it alone. God is with us and wants to inspire us to do the right thing. One simple method that my dad taught me and that helps me a great deal is "PTA"—pray, think, and act:

1. *Pray.* Place yourself in God's presence and ask him to enlighten you.

2. *Think*. Use the wonderful mind God gave you to think through the problem at hand.

3. *Act*. Now act in accordance with what you think God would have you do.

Contact with God at this practical level won't make us spacey or disconnected. Just the opposite is true. We are more fully engaged in our activities when we have the consciousness to stop for a moment, turn our mind toward God, and ask him for guidance and strength. A glance his way helps us know when silence is best, when confrontation is called for, when going the extra mile is the right thing to do.

Regular glances toward God can also help us experience how very much he knows our needs and wants. God wants to love us with personal and intimate gifts. So when we look to him for guidance, his inspiration will point us toward things that will make us truly happy. Maybe you haven't been exercising as you should because you hate running on the treadmill. You can bet that God will inspire you with better, more exciting ideas than treadmills. He knows you. Maybe you will remember that invitation from your friend to join his soccer team. Maybe you will decide to buy a bike. Or perhaps the Holy Spirit will inspire you to buy flowers for your wife and she, through you, will experience God's love in a gift that is a perfect fit.

ACTIVE CONSENT

I can't finish without making a final distinction between the responses of "resignation" and "consent" when our spiritual journey comes on hard times we cannot change. I just got a call from a man I've been in conversation with for a couple of years. Andrew and I first talked when he discovered that his wife—the mother of his three children—had been cheating on him for almost ten years. After going through the normal psychological and spiritual stages of shock, disbelief, anger, and so on, he finally settled a year later into a deep sadness, what he called a "manageable" depression. He was "resigned" to living with something he could never change and would never get over. His resignation was not a willful act. It was a default position of emotional indifference.

When he called me today, I could hear new life in his voice. I knew that he and his wife were going on a marriage renewal retreat, and I figured this must have done it. But according to Andrew, they went and came back in the same exact condition. "So why the joy in your voice?" I asked.

Andrew told me that on the retreat he had decided to start his regular prayer time again. He had no interest in praying about the relationship. He had given up on its ever getting better and didn't expect anything from God in that regard. After all, it wasn't *his* fault. Andrew explained to me, however, with excitement in his voice, that he had felt an unexpected inspiration in prayer to accept his wife's infidelity *as something God had permitted*. Even though Andrew had accepted her apology some time earlier and they were living together again, mostly for the sake of the children, he had never accepted what had happened as being part of a reality God had allowed. In other words, he had resigned himself to the situation, but it was a completely passive response.

The joy Andrew had experienced by actively accepting his situation can be explained by the principle of consent. Consenting to a tragic situation is very different than resigning oneself to it. Have you offered your consent to God's permissive or active will in your life? Have you actively accepted your situation? Have you told God you're confident he will bring forth a greater good out of it?

CONCLUSION

If you broke open these pages because life had taken a tragic twist or because you refused to believe that your blasé status quo was as good as life could be, I'm sure things still don't feel perfect. I do hope, however, that your heart has been bathed with light. I pray that your hope for your own future has been renewed. And I trust that you are testing out or at least contemplating embarking on this journey, away from the self-destructive thought and behavior patterns of yesterday, and toward a new approach to life where faith, hope, and love hold court over our less noble emotions and judgments.

Some of the stories I have recounted here have been of exceptional individuals who have done great things against great odds. Most of us, however, will never have the opportunity to do "big" things. Our lives will be defined by the sum of innumerable and unmemorable decisions, be they good or bad. We will build a life of greater or lesser goodness, joy, and consequence by the way we live the simple routine of each day.

You will remember from this book's introduction that that's what Moe, known as the "last butcher in Little Italy," has done—he has forged a legacy of love in the simplest of ways on Elizabeth Street, just south of Houston Street. If you need a reason to smile, he's the man to go to. If you want someone to treat you as a friend, even if you don't make a purchase, that would be Moe. If you want to witness someone who just keeps going in the face of painful and unavoidable change in his business and neighborhood, stop by Moe's "Albanese Meats" and he will inspire you without doing anything special. You will remember too how contagious the simplicity of Moe's spirit-filled living has been, inspiring owners of the new generation of hip businesses to imitate Moe's goodness. Sean, the owner of Café Habana, not only buys all of his meat products from Moe, but regularly stops in to check on his friend.

The other day I was having breakfast at Café Habana and noticed how happy one of the waitresses was. I asked her how long she had worked at the little restaurant. Her response? "Seven years—it's a great place to work."

"And do you know that your boss keeps Moe, the last butcher in Little Italy, in business by buying all of his meat products from him?" I asked.

"Yes," she said, "but that's the way Sean is, and it's the way he treats all of us too. And besides, Moe has a great product."

So Moe has a great product. I don't doubt that a bit. Not only because I've tried his extra-lean ground beef, but because spirit-filled living, as a way of life, spills over into everything we do. We are better spouses, friends, athletes, business owners . . . and butchers.

Another wonderful man who some might say doesn't do anything exceptional at work teaches me that lesson almost every day. He keeps guard for us, opening and shutting the doors of Studio B in the Fox News Channel offices. About a year ago, I asked Clinton why he's always smiling and kind to everyone who zips in and out of those doors with such important things to do. He didn't give me any particular response that I remember, except that smile and a giggle, but several weeks later he asked me if I had a second to talk. He pulled out of the chest pocket of his blue blazer a sheet of paper. Unfolding it carefully, he pointed gingerly at the title of what at first glance looked like a poem. It read, "This is a wonderful way to start your workday and every day!" Clinton then asked me if I would be willing to "sign up" for his challenge. It was a challenge to pray his prayer every day before work. Part of it went like this:

> Father, I come before you this morning, thanking you for waking me up today. I enter into your courts with thanksgiving and your gates with praise. I declare, Father, that this is the day that you have made, and I shall rejoice and be exceedingly glad in it.
>
> Father, I thank you for this position that you have blessed me with here at _____. I do not take it for granted, but commit myself to performing every task assigned to me as unto you and not unto man.
>
> I will show myself a faithful steward over what you have given me, and in return the blessings of God shall abound in my life.
>
> Give me the strength, Lord, and move in me throughout this day, regardless of circumstances and situations. Help me to operate in the fruit of the Spirit at all times. That means even when I feel like losing control of my tongue, whether it is to speak gossip, to curse, or anything else, I'll speak only those words that bring edification to you, and anything that doesn't edify, I'll cast away from me.

Thank you, Father, for being all that you are to me. I will never find anyone to be as good to me as you are. I love you. In Jesus's name. Amen.

This is the type of down-to-earth spirituality that can transform our lives. I don't know Clinton's whole life story, or even Moe's, but today these men hold out for us, without any airs of presumption, proof of the accessibility of spirit-filled living.

If you have found here ideas that you think you might believe in, now is the time to translate them into action. As a Junior Partner of the Holy Spirit, go forward with determination—notwithstanding a certain trepidation!—knowing there's work to be done that only you can do. You know that your freedom is real. You can use it or abuse it, and the consequences of that decision won't be prevented even by God. Go forward with unshakable confidence, because you have the conviction and the experience that God is on your side. He is there to give you grace in the form of strength, wisdom, prudence, humility, and the audacity to do the right thing. He is also there to contribute to and reward these good choices with the holiness and happiness he desires for you.

The journey I have outlined is one we can spend a lifetime living without ever growing out of. As noted earlier, I have the six steps of the Make Straight the Path process on a bronze plaque on my desk as a constant reminder of the necessary human foundation that prepares me for God's grace. If all else fails, if I mess up or get depressed or if people fail me, I know that renewing these six steps will always be a concrete and real way forward.

When I get stuck and am unable to live the basics of the Christian life (prayer, forgiveness, charity, and so on) I know what to do (see chapter 3). I know I have unconsciously bought into Satan's lies about myself, God, and others that hold me back from preparing my heart to enter into and bask in the Divine Cure. In this regard, the lifelong journey of self-help, leading to God-help, involves special attentiveness to my own failings and limitations, and it is best bolstered by objective friends who can speak frankly to my defects. Whenever I find myself falling into unhealthy habits or having disproportionate, irrational reactions to things or people that bother me, I know I must go back to prayer and ask God to replace lies (about self-worth, real success, and similar concepts) with truth. I can go back to this process of healing every day if necessary, without frustration, because God asks of me only sincerity and perseverance.

And finally, I know that as long as I preserve my desire for friendship with God, I will never tire of the goals of living faith, living hope, and living love. They will continually attract me because my heart was made for them. My spirit, my nature, is congruent with them, and I flourish when they define me. I think back to the various spiritual heroes I've mentioned in these pages—for example, Cynthia and Moe. They have been able to push forward with peace and a smile because their hearts are not set on silly, passing things. Their standard is not the world's mantra of immediate pleasure, power, and fame. Their hearts rest in the right place. Like them, millions of others today have found the narrow road of the gospel—the straight path—that leads to life in abundance. It is my hope that you too are making your way down this path toward the abundant, joyful life God has in mind for you.

God wants us happy. God wants *you* happy. He has given us a way forward.